D0832223

Joe Turner's Come and Gone

by

August Wilson

A SAMUEL FRENCH ACTING EDITION

SAMUEL FRENCH
FOUNDED 1830

New York Hollywood London Toronto
SAMUELFRENCH.COM

ISBN 978-0-573-69142-3   Printed in U.S.A.   #12051

IMPORTANT BILLING AND CREDIT REQUIREMENTS

All producers of *JOE TURNER'S COME AND GONE* *must* give credit to the Author of the Play in all programs distributed in connection with performances of the Play, and in all instances in which the title of the Play appears for the purposes of advertising, publicizing or otherwise exploiting the Play and/or a production. The name of the Author *must* appear on a separate line on which no other name appears, immediately following the title and *must* appear in size of type not less than fifty percent of the size of the title type.

Joe Turner's Come and Gone opened on April 29, 1986 at the Yale Repertory Theatre, Lloyd Richards, Artistic Director, Benjamin Mordecai, Managing Director, in New Haven, Connecticut, with the following cast:

SETH HOLLY.........................Mel Winkler
BERTHA HOLLY...............L. Scott Caldwell
BYNUM WALKER .... Ed Hall
RUTHERFORD SELIG...........Raynor Scheine
JEREMY FURLOW..................... Bo Rucker
HERALD LOOMIS..............Charles S. Dutton
ZONIA LOOMIS.................Cristal Coleman
    and LaJara Henderson at alternate performances
MATTIE CAMPBELL.. Kimberleigh Burroughs
REUBEN MERCER........Casey Lydell Badger
    and LaMar James Fedrick at alternate performances
MOLLY CUNNINGHAM........ Kimberly Scott
MARTHA PENTECOST.........Angela Bassett

Director: Lloyd Richards
Set Design: Scott Bradley
Costume Design: Pamela Peterson
Lighting Design: Michael Gianiti
Musical Direction: Dwight Andrews
Sound Design: Matthew Wiener
Production Stage Manager: Margaret Adair
Stage Manager: Ethan Ruber
Casting: Meg Simon/Fran Kumin

The Yale Repertory Theatre production of *Joe Turner's Come and Gone* opened on October 2, 1987 at the Arena Stage, Zelda Fichandler, Producing Director, William Stewart, Managing Director, Douglas C. Wager, Associate Producing Director, in Washington, D.C., with the following cast:

SETH HOLLY........................Mel Winkler
BERTHA HOLLY................L. Scott Caldwell
BYNUM WALKER........................ Ed Hall
RUTHERFORD SELIG...........Raynor Scheine
JEREMY FURLOW..................... Bo Rucker
HERALD LOOMIS..................Delroy Lindo
ZONIA LOOMIS................. Kippen Hay and
    Kellie S. Williams at alternate performances
MATTIE CAMPBELL........ Kimberleigh Aarn
REUBEN MERCER...........LaFontaine Oliver
    and Vincent Prevost at alternate
    performances
MOLLY CUNNINGHAM........ Kimberly Scott
MARTHA PENTECOST.........Angela Bassett

Director: Lloyd Richards
Set Design: Scott Bradley
Costume Design: Pamela Peterson
Lighting Design: Michael Gianiti
Musical Direction: Dwight Andrews
Stage Manager: Karen L. Carpenter
Casting Consultants: Meg Simon/Fran Kumin

Joe Turner's Come and Gone opened on March 27, 1988, at the Ethel Barrymore Theatre on Broadway in New York City, with the following cast:

SETH HOLLY	Mel Winkler
BERTHA HOLLY	L. Scott Caldwell
BYNUM WALKER	Ed Hall
RUTHERFORD SELIG	Raynor Scheine
JEREMY FURLOW	Bo Rucker
HERALD LOOMIS	Delroy Lindo
ZONIA LOOMIS	Jamilla Perry
MATTIE CAMPBELL	Kimberleigh Aarn
REUBEN MERCER	Richard Habersham
MOLLY CUNNINGHAM	Kimberly Scott
MARTHA PENTECOST	Angela Bassett

Producers: Elliot Martin, Vy Higgensen, Ken Wydro
Director: Lloyd Richards
Musical Director: Dwight Andrews
Costume Designer: Pam Peterson
Lighting Designer: Michael Gianiti
Scenic Designer: Scott Bradley
Production Stage Manager: Karen L. Carpenter
Assistant Stage Manager: Eliott Woodruff
General Manager: Steve Goldstein, Joseph Harris Associates
Press Representative: Jeff Richards Associates
Casting: Simon & Kumin

CHARACTERS

(in order of appearance)

SETH HOLLY – owner of the boarding house
BERTHA HOLLY – his wife
BYNUM WALKER – a root worker
RUTHERFORD SELIG – a peddler
JEREMY FURLOW – a resident
HERALD LOOMIS – a resident
ZONIA LOOMIS – his daughter
MATTIE CAMPBELL – a resident
REUBEN MERCER – a boy who lives next door
MOLLY CUNNINGHAM – a resident
MARTHA LOOMIS – Herald Loomis's wife

THE PLAY

It is August in Pittsburgh, 1911. The sun falls out of heaven like a stone. The fires of the steel mill rage with a combined sense of industry and progress. Barges loaded with coal and iron ore trudge up the river to the mill towns that dot the Monongahela and return with fresh, hard, gleaming steel. The city flexes its muscles. Men throw countless bridges across the rivers, lay roads and carve tunnels through the hills sprouting with houses.

From the deep and near South the sons and daughters of newly freed African slaves wander into the city. Isolated, cut off from memory, having forgotten the names of the gods and only guessing at their faces, they arrive dazed and stunned, their hearts kicking in their chest with a song worth singing. They arrive carrying Bibles and guitars, their pockets lined with dust and fresh hope, marked men and women seeking to scrape from the narrow crooked cobbles and the fiery blasts of the coke furnace a way of bludgeoning and shaping the malleable parts of themselves into a new identity as free men of definite and sincere worth.

Foreigners in a strange land, they carry as part and parcel of their baggage a long line of separation and dispersement which informs their sensibilities and marks their conduct as they search for ways to reconnect, to reassemble, to give clear and luminous meaning to the song which is both a wail and a whelp of joy.

SET

August, 1911. A boarding house in Pittsburgh. At right is a kitchen. On the right side of the kitchen is a sink with running water and a drainboard, and an icebox. A window over the icebox looks out onto the porch. Between the window and the porch door is a hook for hats. The upstage wall of the kitchen is dominated by a large fireplace with a mantle. In the fireplace is a coal stove with an oven and six burners. On the stove is a pot of coffee, a pan of grits, and a saucepan of gravy. In the oven is a pan of biscuits. A shelf over the stove holds hot pads, serving utensils, salt and pepper shakers, butter dish and sugar bowl. To the right of the stove is a small table for preparing biscuits; to the left is a small table (upstage center), which holds all of the dishes, napkins, and utensils for serving food. In the center of the kitchen is a long dining table, surrounded by five pressback wooden chairs on the stage right, left, and upstage sides. A long bench for additional seating is placed downstage of the kitchen table. A long gas fixture with a lamp at either end hangs over the table.

Two doors open off the kitchen. The stage right door leads to a small porch with a railing and steps leading down to the yard. The upstage right door leads to SETH's and BERTHA's bedroom. An archway upstage center leads into the kitchen pantry directly upstage and the hallway towards stage left; another archway with a sliding door is center stage and connects the kitchen and the parlor. The sliding door is closed.

At left is the parlor. The parlor is furnished with a round table draped with a decorative cloth at center, surrounded by a love seat on the stage left side, an upholstered arm chair upstage, and side chair stage right of it. A gas lamp hangs over the table. There is a large shuttered window in the stage left wall above the love seat, and a rooms-to-let sign hangs in it.

A large archway leads from the upstage of the parlor into the front hall foyer. The front door upstage left opens into the front hall which gives access to the parlor and the stairs leading to the upstairs rooms. In this hallway upstage of the center arch is a mirrored sideboard, with hooks for hats and coats.

There is a stone pathway leading from the porch steps stage right to the cellar door, downstage center. Offstage, down right leads to the outhouse and vegetable garden, and upstage right leads to SETH's workshop. The house is framed by a wooden fence upstage, on either side of the house, and over the house is the skyline of Pittsburgh: factories, smokestacks, and a train trestle bridge.

ACT I

Scene 1

SOUND: musical montage fades up: children singing and clapping in time in the yard, stage right; cross fades to a guitarist and a harmonica player making music in front of the house, stage left; cross fades to BYNUM singing "They tell me Joe Turner's come and gone ..." from both sides of the stage. At end of second verse, LIGHTS: fade to black with SOUND: train whistle sounds from the distance stage left. Train approaches, crosses trestle bridge over stage, and fades into the distance stage right as LIGHTS: fade up on the kitchen. BERTHA enters from the pantry with a stack of plates, crosses to the upstage center table and puts them down. She busies herself with breakfast preparation. SETH enters stage left, looking back over his shoulder toward the yard. He laughs, shakes his head and enters the kitchen through the porch door. SETH is in his early fifties. Born of Northern free parents, a skilled craftsman and owner of the boardinghouse, he has a stability and completeness that none of the other characters have. BERTHA is five years his junior. Married for over twenty-five years, she has learned how to negotiate around SETH's apparent orneries.

SETH. (*At the window, laughing.*) If that ain't the damnest thing I seen. Look here, Bertha.

BERTHA. I done seen Bynum out there with them pigeons before.

SETH. Naw ... naw ... look at this. That pigeon flopped out of Bynum's hand and he about to have a fit.

(BERTHA crosses over to the window. SETH stands above her and points out to the yard.)

SETH. He down there on his hands and knees behind that bush looking all over for that pigeon and it on the other side of the yard. See it over there?

(BERTHA moves away toward the stove. SETH stops her and gives her a kiss on the cheek.)

BERTHA. Comeon and get your breakfast and leave that man alone. *(Crosses to the stove, stirs the grits and gravy, and picks up the butter dish from the shelf over the stove.)*

SETH. *(Drawn back to the window, looks offstage right.)* Look at him ... he still looking. He ain't seen it yet. *(He hangs his hat on the hook over the icebox, puts his lunch pail and work gloves down on the icebox.)* All that old mumbo jumbo nonsense. I don't know why I put up with it.

BERTHA. *(Sets the butter dish center on the kitchen table.)* You don't say nothing when he bless the house.

(SETH picks up the salt and pepper shakers from the shelf over the stove, puts them down at the center of the kitchen table.)

SETH. I just go along with that cause of you. You around here sprinkling salt all over the place ... got pennies lines up across the threshold ... all that heebie-jeebie stuff. I just put up with that cause of you. I don't pay that kind of stuff no mind. But you going down there to the church and wanna come home and sprinkle salt all over the place. (*Goes back to the window, looks out offstage right.*)

BERTHA. (*Picks up the salt shaker, shakes some salt into her left hand.*) It don't hurt none. I can't say if it help ... (*Throws salt over her right shoulder.*) but it don't hurt none.

(*BERTHA picks up hot pads, opens oven door, and tests biscuits with finger.*)

SETH. Look at him. He done found that pigeon and now he's talking to it.

BERTHA. These biscuits be ready in a minute.

(*BERTHA closes oven door, rises, puts hot pads down on stove shelf.*)

SETH. He done drew a big circle with that stick and now he's dancing around. I know he'd better not ...

(*SETH bolts from the window, rushes to the back door, and steps out onto the porch.*)

SETH. Hey Bynum! Don't be hopping around stepping on my vegetables. Hey Bynum ... Watch where you stepping!

BERTHA. (*Turns to him.*) Seth, leave that man alone.

SETH. (*Steps back into kitchen, closes porch door, turns to her.*) I don't care how much he be dancing around ... just don't be stepping in my vegetables. Man got my garden all messed up now ... planting them weeds out there ... burying them pigeons and whatnot.

BERTHA. (*Picks up sugar bowl from shelf over stove, sets at center of kitchen table.*) Bynum don't bother nobody. He ain't even thinking about your vegetables.

SETH. I know he ain't! That's why he out there stepping on them. (*Washes his hands at the kitchen sink.*)

BERTHA. What Mr. Johnson say down there?

SETH. I told him if I had the tools I could go out here and find me four or five fellows and open up my own shop instead of working for Mr. Olowski. Get me four or five fellows and teach them how to make pots and pans. One man making ten pots is five men making fifty. (*Dries hands on towel over sink.*) He told me he'd think about it.

BERTHA. Well maybe he'll come to see it your way.

SETH. (*Stops drying hands, turns to her.*) He wanted me to sign over the house to him. You know what I thought of that idea.

BERTHA. He'll come to see you're right.

(*BERTHA picks up the hot pads, opens the oven and takes out a pan of biscuits. She puts the pan down on the stove burner and dishes up SETH's breakfast.*)

SETH. I'm going up and talk to Sam Green. There's more than one way to skin a cat. I'm going up and talk to him. See if he got more sense than Mr. Johnson. I can't get nowhere working for Mr. Olowski and selling Selig five or six pots on the side. I'm going up and see Sam Green. See if he loan me the money. (*He crosses back to the window.*) Now he got that cup. He done killed that pigeon and now he's putting its blood in that little cup. I believe he drink that blood.

BERTHA. (*Sets his breakfast on the kitchen table at the stage right place.*) Seth Holly, what is wrong with you this morning. Comeon and get your breakfast so you can go to bed. You know Bynum don't be drinking no pigeon blood.

SETH. (*Rises, and turns to her.*) I don't know what he do.

BERTHA. Well watch him then. He's gonna dig a little hole and bury that pigeon. Thern he's gonna pray over that blood ... pour it on top ... mark out his circle and come on into the house.

(*BERTHA goes back to the stove and picks up the coffee pot. SETH turns back, looks out the window.*)

SETH. That's what he doing ... he pouring that blood on top.

BERTHA. (*Pours SETH's coffee at the kitchen table.*) When they gonna put you back working daytime. Told me two months ago he was gonna put you back working daytime.

SETH. (*Sits in the stage right kitchen chair, unrolls his utensils from the napkin.*) That's what Mr. Olowski told me. I got to wait till he say when. He tell me what to do. I don't tell him. Drive me crazy to speculate on the man's wishes when he don't know what he want to do himself.

BERTHA. Well, I wish he go ahead and put you back working daytime. This working all hours of the night don't make no sense. (*Puts the coffee pot back on the stove.*)

SETH. (*Butters biscuit.*) It don't make no sense for that boy to run out of of here and get drunk so they lock him up either.

BERTHA. (*Turns to him.*) Who? Who they got locked up for being drunk?

SETH. That boy that's staying upstairs ... Jeremy. I stopped down there on Logan Street on my way home from work and one of the fellows told me about it. Say he seen it when they arrested him.

BERTHA. I was wondering why I ain't seen him this morning.

SETH. You know I don't put up with that. I told him when he came ...

(*BYNUM enters from the yard through the porch door, carrying his basket of weeds. He puts the basket down at his place on the kitchen table, upstage left, and continues into the hallway. He hangs his hat on the hook at the sideboard. BERTHA picks up a place setting for him. BYNUM is in his early sixties, a conjure man, or rootworker, and gives the impression of always being in control of everything. Nothing ever bothers him. He seems to be lost in a world of his own making and to swallow any adversity or interference with his grand design.*)

SETH. What you doing bringing them weeds in my house? Out there stepping on my vegetables and now wanna carry them weeds in my house.

BYNUM. (*Crosses to the sink and washes his hands.*) Morning, Seth. Morning, Sister Bertha.

(*BERTHA distastefully picks up BYNUM's basket, places it on the floor at the upstage left corner of the kitchen. She picks up a place setting for BYNUM.*)

SETH. Messing up my garden growing them things out there. I ought to go out there and pull up all them weeds.

BERTHA. (*Crosses to the upstage left place, puts down place setting.*) Some gal was by here this morning, Bynum. You was out there in the yard ... I told her to come back later. (*Picks up spatula, dishes up a biscuit for BYNUM.*)

BYNUM. (*To SETH.*) You look sick. What's the matter, you ain't eating right? (*Sits at the upstage left chair.*)

SETH. What if I was sick? You ain't getting near me with none of that stuff.

(*BERTHA sets a plate with a biscuit on the table in front of BYNUM.*)

BYNUM. My ... my ... Bertha, your biscuits getting fatter and fatter.

(*BERTHA smiles, crosses to stove, picks up coffee pot. BYNUM begins to eat the biscuit.*)

BYNUM. Where Jeremy? I don't see him around this morning. He usually be around riffing and raffing on Saturday morning.

(*BERTHA pours BYNUM's coffee at the kitchen table.*)

SETH. I know where he at. I know just where he at. They got him down there in the jail. Getting drunk and acting a fool. He down there where he belong with all that foolishness.

(BERTHA puts the coffee pot down on the stove, the hot pads on the stove shelf. She cleans up the flour, and biscuit makings from the upstage right table.)

BYNUM. Mr. Piney's boys got him, huh? They ain't gonna do nothing but hold on to him for a little while. He's gonna be back here hungrier than a mule directly.

SETH. I don't go for all that carrying on and such. This is a respectable house. I don't have no drunkards or fools around here.

BYNUM. That boy got a lot of country in him. He ain't been up here but two weeks. It's gonna take awhile before he can work that country out of him.

(BERTHA takes the flour cannister and baking powder tin to the pantry cupboard. She puts them away, and then sorts through her mending basket on the pantry shelf.)

SETH. These niggers coming up here with that old backward country style of living. It's hard enough now without all that ignorant kind of acting. Ever since slavery got over with there ain't been nothing but foolish acting niggers. Word get out they need men to work in the mill and put in these roads ... and niggers drop everything and head North looking for freedom. They don't know the white fellows looking too. White fellows coming from all over the world. White fellow come over and in six months got more that what I got. But these niggers keep on coming. Walking ... riding ... carrying their Bibles. That boy done carried a guitar all the way from North Carolina. What he gonna find out? What he gonna do with that guitar? This is the city.

(*RUTHERFORD SELIG knocks on the porch door. SETH goes to answer the door.*)

SETH. Niggers coming up from the backwoods ... coming up here from the country carrying Bibles and guitars looking for freedom. They got a rude awakening. (*Opens the door.*) Ho! Forgot you was coming today. Comeon in.

(*RUTHERFORD SELIG enters the kitchen, past SETH. About SETH's age, he is a thin white man with greasy hair. As a peddler, he supplies SETH with the new materials to make pots and pans which he then peddles door to door in the mill towns along the river. He keeps a list of his customers as they move about and is known in the various communities as the People Finder. He carries squares of sheet metal under his arm.*)

BYNUM. If it ain't Rutherford Selig ... the People Finder himself.
SELIG. What say there, Bynum?
BYNUM. I say about my shiny man. You got to tell me something. I done give you my dollar ... I'm looking to get a report.
SELIG. (*Turns to SETH, hands him the sheet metal squares.*) I got eight here, Seth.

SETH. (*Takes the sheet metal.*) What is this? (*Inspects the metal, flexing it.*) What you giving me here? What I'm gonna do with this?

SELIG. I need some dustpans. Everybody asking me about dustpans.

SETH. Gonna cost you fifteen cents apiece. And ten cents to put a handle on them.

SELIG. I'll give you twenty cents apiece with the handles.

SELIG. Alright. But I ain't gonna give you but fifteen cents for the sheet metal.

SELIG. It's twenty-five cents apiece for the metal. That's what we agreed on.

SETH. (*Holds the sheet metal out to SELIG.*) This low grade sheet metal. They ain't worth but a dime. I'm doing you a favor giving you fifteen cents. (*Becoming more argumentative.*) You know this metal ain't worth no twenty-five cents. Don't come talking that twenty-five cents stuff to me over no low grade sheet metal.

SETH. Alright, fifteen cents apiece. Just make me some dustpans out of them.

(*SETH exits with the sheet metal out the porch door, towards his workshop. BERTHA enters the kitchen, crosses to the upstage center table.*)

BERTHA. Sit on down there, Selig. Get you a cup of coffee and a biscuit.

(*SELIG puts his hat down on the kitchen table, sits in the upstage right chair. BERTHA picks up a place setting for SELIG.*)

BYNUM. Where you coming from this time?

(BERTHA puts down SELIG's setting in front of him on the kitchen table, distastefully picks up his hat and hangs it on the back of the upstage center chair.)

SELIG. I been upriver. All along the Monongahela. Past Rankin and all up around Little Washington.

(BERTHA gets the coffee pot from the stove and pours SELIG's coffee at the kitchen table.)

BYNUM. Did you find anybody?

SELIG. I found Sadie Jackson up in Braddock. Her mother's staying down there in Scotchbottom say she hadn't heard from her and she didn't know where she was at. I found her up in Braddock on Enoch Street. She bought a frying pan from me.

(BERTHA puts the coffee pot down on the stove, dishes up a biscuit for SELIG.)

BYNUM. You around here finding everybody how come you ain't found my shiny man.

SELIG. The only shiny man I saw was the nigras working on the road gang with the sweat glistening on them.

BYNUM. Naw, you'd be able to tell this fellow. He shine like new money.

SELIG. Well, I done told you I can't find nobody without a name.

BERTHA. *(Puts the plate with the biscuit down in front of SELIG.)* Here go one of these hot biscuits, Selig.

(*SELIG slices his biscuit, puts a pat of butter inside, folds it up in his handkerchief, and puts it in his pocket.*)

BYNUM. This fellow don't have no name. I call him John cause it was up around Johnstown where I seen him. I ain't even so sure he's one special fellow. That shine could pass on to anybody. He could be anybody shining.

SELIG. Well, what's he look like beside being shiny. There's lots of shiny nigras.

(*SELIG takes his pipe out of his pocket, lights it, and looks around for a place to put the match. BERTHA picks up an ashtray from the stove shelf, and puts it down in front of SELIG. He places the match in it. She picks up the mixing bowl from the upstage right table and takes it to the sink.*)

BYNUM. He's just a man I seen out on the road. He ain't had no special look. Just a man walking toward me on the road. He come up and asked me which way the road went. I told him everything I knew about the road, where it went and all, and he asked me did I have anything to eat 'cause he was hungry. Say he ain't had nothing to eat in three days. Well, I never be out there on the road without a piece of dried meat. Or an orange or an apple. So I give this fellow an orange. He take and eat that orange and told me to come and go along the road a little ways with him, that he had something he wanted to show me. He had a look about him made me wanna go with him, see what he gonna show me.

We walked on a bit and it's getting kind of far from where I met him when it come up on me all of a sudden, we wasn't going the way he had come from, we was going back my way. Since he said he ain't knew nothing about the road, I asked him about this. He say he had a voice inside him telling him which way to go and if I come and go along with him he was gonna show me the Secret of Life. Quite naturally I followed him. A fellow that's gonna show you the Secret of Life ain't to be taken lightly. We get near this bend in the road...

(*SETH enters with an assortment of pots, crosses to SELIG.*)

SETH. I got six here, Selig.

SELIG. Wait a minute, Seth. Bynum's telling me about the secret of life. Go ahead Bynum, I wanna hear this.

BYNUM. We get near this bend in the road and he told me to hold out my hands. Then he rubbed them together with his and I look down and see they had blood on them ...

(*SETH drops the pots loudly on the kitchen floor and exits out the porch door.*)

BYNUM. I look down and see they had blood on them. Told me to take and rub it all over me, say that was a way of cleaning myself. Then we went around the bend in that road. Got around that bend and it seem like all of a sudden we ain't in the same place. Turn around that bend and everything look like it was twice as big as it was. The trees and everything bigger than life. Sparrows big as eagles. I turned around to look at this fellow and he had this light coming out of him. I had to cover up my eyes to

keep from being blinded. He shining like new money with
that light. He shined until all the light seemed like it
seeped out of him and then he was gone and I was by
myself in this strange place where everything was bigger
than life.

I wandered around there looking for that road, trying to
find my way back from this big place, and I looked over
and seen my daddy standing there. He was the same size he
always was, except for his hands and his mouth. He had a
great big old mouth that looked like it took up his whole
face and his hands were as big as hams. Look like they was
too big to carry around. My daddy called me to him. Said
he had been thinking about me and it grieved him to see
me in the world carrying other people's songs and not
having one of my own. Told me he was gonna show me
how to find my song. Then he carried me further into this
big place until we come to this ocean. Then he showed me
something I ain't got words to tell you. If you stand to
witness it, you done seen something there. I stayed in that
place awhile and my daddy taught me the meaning of this
thing that I had seen and showed me how to find my song.
I asked him about the shiny man and he tole me he was the
One Who Goes Before and Shows the Way. Say there was
lots of shiny men and if I ever saw one again before I died
that I would know that my song had been accepted and
worked its full power in the world and I could lay down and
die a happy man. A man who done left his mark on life.
On the way people cling to each other out of the truth they
find in themselves. Then he showed me how to get back to
the road. I came out to where everything was its own size
and I had my song. I had the Binding Song. I choose that
song because that's what I seen most when I was traveling

... people walking away and leaving one another. So I takes the power of my song and binds them together.

(*SETH enters from the yard carrying a burlap sack full of cabbages and tomatoes.*)

BYNUM. Been binding people ever since. That's why they call me Bynum. Just like glue I sticks people together.

(*BERTHA laughs, turns to the sink, and starts to wash the dishes.*)

SETH. Maybe they ain't supposed to be stuck sometimes. You ever think of that?

BERTHA. Oh, I don't do it lightly. It costs me a piece of myself everytime I do. I'm a Binder of What Clings. You got to find out if they cling first. You can't bind what don't cling.

SELIG. Well, now is that the Secret of Life? I thought you said he was gonna show you the secret of life.

BYNUM. Oh, he showed me alright. But you still got to figure it out. Can't nobody figure it out for you. You got to come to it on your own. That's why I'm looking for the shiny man.

SELIG. (*Rises, turns to SETH.*) Well, I'll keep my eye out for him. What you got there, Seth.

SETH. (*Hands him the burlap bag.*) Here go some cabbage and tomatoes. I got some greenbeans coming in real nice. I'm gonna take and start me a grapevine out there next year. Butera say he gonna give me a piece of his vine and I'm gonna start that out there.

SELIG. (*Takes his money out of his shoulder bag to pay SETH.*) How many of them pots you got?

SETH. (*Picks up pots from floor.*) I got six. (*Rapidly.*) That's six dollars minus eight on top of fifteen for the sheet metal come to a dollar twenty out the six dollars leave me four dollars and eighty cents.

SELIG. (*Unable to keep up with him, counts out the money and hands it to SETH.*) There's four dollars ... and ... eighty cents.

SETH. (*Hands pots to SELIG.*) How many of them dustpans you want?

SELIG. (*Puts leftover bills and coins in shoulder bag.*) As many as you can make out them sheets.

SETH. You can use that many? I get to cutting on them sheets figuring how to make them dustpans ... ain't no telling how many I'm liable to come up with.

SELIG. I can use them and you can make me some more next time.

SETH. (*Pockets money.*) Alright, I'm gonna hold you to that now.

SELIG. (*Crosses to porch door.*) Thanks for the biscuit, Bertha.

BERTHA. You know you welcome anytime, Selig.

SETH. Which way you heading?

SELIG. (*Turns back to SETH.*) Going down to Wheeling. All through West Virginia there. I'll be back Saturday. They putting in new roads down that way. Makes traveling easier.

SETH. That's what I hear. All around here too. Got a fellow staying here working on that road by the Brady Street Bridge.

SELIG. Yeah, it's gonna make traveling real nice. Thanks for the cabbage, Seth. I'll see you on Saturday.

(*Exits with pots and burlap sack, closes porch door as he goes.*)

SETH. (*Turns to BYNUM.*) Why you wanna start all that nonsense talk with that man? All that shiny man nonsense.

BYNUM. You know it ain't no nonsense. Bertha know it ain't no nonsense. I don't know if Selig know or not.

(*SETH crosses to stage right chair, sits fuming. BERTHA dries dishes.*)

BERTHA. (*Turns to SETH.*) Seth, when you get to making them dustpans ... make me a coffee pot.

SETH. What's the matter with your coffee? Ain't nothing wrong with your coffee. Don't she make some good coffee, Bynum?

BYNUM. I ain't worried about the coffee. I know she makes some good biscuits.

SETH. I ain't studying no coffee pot, woman. You heard me tell the man I was gonna cut as many dustpans as them sheets will make ... and all of a sudden you want a coffee pot.

BERTHA. (*Crosses to the pantry to put away the mixing bowl.*) Man, hush up and go on and make me that coffee pot.

(*SETH laughs. JEREMY enters the kitchen through the porch door. About twenty-five, he gives the impression that he has the world in his hand, that he can meet life's challenges head on. He smiles a lot. He is a proficient guitar player, though his spirit has yet to be molded into song.*)

BYNUM. I hear Mr. Piney's boys had you.

JEREMY. Fined me two dollars for nothing! Ain't done nothing.

SETH. (*Angrily.*) I told you when you come on here everybody know my house. Know these is respectable quarters. I don't put up with no foolishness. Everybody know Seth Holly keep a good house. Was my daddy's house. This house been a decent house for a long time.

JEREMY. I ain't done nothing, Mr. Seth. I stopped by the Workmens Club and got me a bottle, me and Roper Lee from Alabama.

(*BERTHA comes in to the kitchen, JEREMY takes his cap off when he sees her.*)

JEREMY. Had us a half pint. We was fixing to cut that half in two when they come up on us. Asked us if we was working. We told them we was putting in the road over yonder and that it was our payday. They snatched hold of us to get that two dollars. Me and Roper Lee ain't even had a chance to take a drink when they grabbed us. (*Goes to the sink and washes his hands.*)

SETH. I don't go for all that kind of carrying on.

BERTHA. Leave the boy alone, Seth. You know the police do that. Figure there's too many people out on the street they take some of them off. You know that.

SETH. I ain't gonna have folks talking.

BERTHA. Ain't nobody talking nothing. That's all in your head. You want some grits and biscuits, Jeremy?

JEREMY. Thank you, Miss Bertha.

(*BERTHA dishes up JEREMY's breakfast.*)

JEREMY. They didn't give us a thing to eat last night. I'll take one of them big bowls if you don't mind.

(*There is a knock at the door. BYNUM sings "They tell me Joe Turner's come and gone ..." SETH goes to answer it. BERTHA sets JEREMY's breakfast downstage right on the kitchen table. He sits down at the stage right end of the bench and begins to eat voraciously. BERTHA pours JEREMY's coffee. As LOOMIS speaks, BYNUM stops singing.*)

LOOMIS. Me and my daughter looking for a place to stay, Mister.

(*HERALD LOOMIS steps over the threshold. He wears a long wool deacon's overcoat and a hat pulled down over his forehead. LOOMIS is thirty-two years old. He is at times possessed. A man driven not by the hell hounds that seemingly bay at his heels, but by his search for a world that speaks to something about himself. He is unable to harmonize the forces that swirl around him, and seeks to recreate the world into one thing that contains his image.*)

LOOMIS. You got a sign say you got rooms.

(*SETH stares at LOOMIS, sizing him up.*)

LOOMIS. Mister if you ain't got no rooms we can go somewhere else.
SETH. (*Suspiciously.*) How long you plan on staying?

LOOMIS. Don't know. Two weeks or more maybe.

SETH. (*Reluctantly.*) It's two dollars a week for the room. We serve meals twice a day. It's two dollars for room and board. Pay up in advance.

(*LOOMIS brings ZONIA, his eleven-year-old daughter, over the threshold downstage of him. She is dressed neatly although her clothes are too small for her, and wears a battered straw hat. ZONIA carries a bundle. LOOMIS reaches into this pocket.*)

SETH. It's a dollar extra for the girl.

(*BERTHA goes to the sliding door and opens it.*)

LOOMIS. The girl sleep in the same room.

SETH. Well, do she eat off the same plate? We serve meals twice a day. That's a dollar extra for the food.

LOOMIS. Ain't got no extra dollar.

(*LOOMIS sees BERTHA, and brings ZONIA forward to stand in front of him. He puts his hands on her shoulders.*)

LOOMIS. I was planning on asking your Missus if she could help out with the cooking and cleaning and whatnot.

SETH. (*Unrelenting.*) Her helping out don't put no food on the table. I need that dollar to buy some food.

LOOMIS. I'll give you fifty cents more. She don't eat much.

SETH. Okay ... but fifty cents don't buy but half a portion.

BERTHA. (*Admonishes him.*) Seth, she can help me out. Let her help me out. I can use some help.

SETH. (*Unwillingly.*) Well, that's two dollars for the week. Pay up in advance. Saturday to Saturday. You wanna stay on then its two more come Saturday.

(*LOOMIS pays SETH the money. SETH crosses to the kitchen through the hallway. BERTHA backs into the kitchen to below the stove. LOOMIS follows her, leading ZONIA by the hand, and stops at center stage.*)

BERTHA. My name's Bertha.

(*SETH enters the kitchen, stands near the upstage right table.*)

BERTHA. That's my husband, Seth. (*Gestures to BYNUM and JEREMY in turn.*) You got Bynum and Jeremy over there.

LOOMIS. Ain't nobody else live here?

BERTHA. They the only ones live here now. People come and go. They the only ones here now. (*Kindly, to ZONIA.*) You want a cup of coffee and a biscuit?

(*ZONIA smiles.*)

LOOMIS. (*Steps between ZONIA and BERTHA, pulls ZONIA behind him.*) We done ate this morning.

BYNUM. Where you coming from, mister ... I didn't get your name.

LOOMIS. Name's Herald Loomis (*Brings ZONIA forward.*) This is my daughter, Zonia.

BYNUM. (*Insistently.*) Where you coming from?

LOOMIS. Come from all over. Whichever way the road takes us that's the way we go.

JEREMY. If you looking for a job, I'm working putting in that road down there by the bridge. They can't get enough mens. Always looking to take somebody on.

LOOMIS. I'm looking for a woman named Martha Loomis. That's my wife. Got married legal with the papers and all.

SETH. I don't know nobody named Loomis. I know some Marthas but I don't know no Loomis.

BYNUM. You got to see Rutherford Selig if you wanna find somebody. Selig's the People Finder. Rutherford Selig's a First Class People Finder.

JEREMY. (*Unsure.*) I don't know. I might have seen her.

BYNUM. You got to see Rutherford Selig. You give him one dollar to get her name on his list ... and after she get her name on his list Rutherford Selig will go right on out there and find her. I got him looking for somebody for me.

LOOMIS. You say he find people. How you find him?

BYNUM. You just missed him. He's gone down river now. You got to wait till Saturday. He's gone down river with his pots and pans. He come to see Seth on Saturdays. You got to wait till then.

SETH. Comeon, I'll show you to your room.

(SETH starts down the hallway and goes up the stairs. LOOMIS hesitates and then follows him, leading ZONIA by the hand. BERTHA crosses quickly to the sliding door and waves to ZONIA as she gets to the stair landing. ZONIA shyly waves back. They exit up

the stairs as BERTHA closes the sliding door, and laughs.)

JEREMY. *(Sits in SETH's chair.)* Miss Bertha, I'll take that biscuit you was gonna give that fellow, if you don't mind.

(BERTHA goes to stove and picks up biscuit with spatula.)

JEREMY. Say Mr. Bynum, they got somebody like that around here sure enough? Somebody what find people?

(JEREMY picks up SETH's leftover biscuit. BERTHA brings the fresh biscuit to the table and puts it on JEREMY's plate. She slaps his hand holding SETH's biscuit. He drops it. BERTHA clears SETH's breakfast dishes to the sink. JEREMY moves his plate to him and eats the fresh biscuit.)

BYNUM. Rutherford Selig. He go around selling his pots and pans and every house he come to he write down the name and address of whoever lives there. So if you looking for somebody, quite naturally you go and see him ... cause he's the only one who know where everybody live at.

JEREMY. I ought to have him look for this old gal I used to know. It be nice to see her again.

BERTHA. *(Stacks SELIG's dishes.)* Jeremy, today's the day for you to pull them sheets off the bed and set them outside your door. I'll set you out some clean ones. *(Clears dishes to the sink and washes them.)*

BYNUM. Mr. Piney's boys done ruined your good time last night, Jeremy ... what you planning for tonight?

JEREMY. They got me scared to go out, Mr. Bynum. They might grab me again.

BYNUM. You ought to take your guitar and go down to Seefus. Seefus got a gambling place down there on Wylie Avenue. You ought to take your guitar and go down there. They got guitar contest down there.

JEREMY. I don't play no contest, Mr. Bynum. Had one of them white fellows cure me of that. I ain't been nowhere near a contest since.

BYNUM. White fellow beat you playing guitar?

JEREMY. Naw, he ain't beat me. I was sitting at home just fixing to sit down and eat when somebody come up to my house and got me. Told me there's a white fellow say he was gonna give a prize to the best guitar player he could find. I take up my guitar and go down there and somebody had gone up and got Bobo Smith and brought him down there. Him and another fellow called Hooter. Old Hooter couldn't play no guitar, he do more hollering than playing, but Bobo could go at it awhile.

This fellow standing there say he the one that was gonna give the prize and me and Bobo started playing for him. Bobo play something and then I'd try to play something better than what he played. Old Hooter, he just hollor and bang at the guitar. Man was the worse guitar player I ever seen. So me and Bobo played and after awhile I seen where he was getting the attention of this white fellow. He'd play something and while he was playing it he be slapping on the side of the guitar, and that made it sound like he was playing more than he was. So I started doing it too. White fellow ain't knew no difference. He ain't knew as much about guitar playing as Hooter did.

After we play while, the white fellow called us to him and said he couldn't make up his mind, say all three of us was the best guitar player and we'd have to split the prize between us. Then he give us twenty-five cents. That's eight cents apiece and a penny on the side. That cured me of playing contest to this day.

BYNUM. Seefus ain't like that. Seefus give a whole dollar and a drink of whiskey.

JEREMY. What night they be down there?

BYNUM. Be down there every night. Music don't know no certain night.

BERTHA. (*Stacks JEREMY's dishes.*) You go down to Seefus with them people and you liable to end up in a raid and go to jail sure enough. I don't know why Bynum tell you that. (*Stacks BYNUM's dishes.*)

BYNUM. That's where the music at. That's where the people at. The people down there making music and enjoying themselves. Somethings is worth taking the chance going to jail about.

BERTHA. (*Clears both sets of dishes to the sink and washes them.*) Jeremy ain't got no business going down there.

JEREMY. They got some women down there, Mr. Bynum?

BYNUM. Oh, they got women down there sure. They got women everywhere. Women be where the man is so they can find each other.

JEREMY. Some them old gals come out there where we be putting in that road. Hanging around there trying to snatch somebody.

BYNUM. How come some of them ain't snatched hold of you?

JEREMY. I don't want them kind. Them desperate kind. Ain't nothing worse than a desperate woman. Tell them you gonna leave them and they get to crying and carrying on. That just make you want to get away quicker. They get to cutting up your clothes and things trying to keep you staying. Desperate women ain't nothing but trouble for a man.

(*SETH enters from the stairs. JEREMY quickly ducks out of his seat and sits back down on the bench.*)

SETH. Something ain't setting right with that fellow.

BERTHA. (*Stops washing dishes and turns to him.*) What's wrong with him? What he say?

SETH. I take him up there and try to talk to him and he ain't for no talking. Say he been traveling ... coming over from Ohio. Say he a deacon in the church. Say he looking for Martha Pentecost. Talking about that's his wife.

BERTHA. How you know it's the same Martha? Could be talking about anybody. Lots of people named Martha.

SETH. You see that little girl? I didn't hook it up till he said it, but that little girl look just like her. Ask Bynum. (*To BYNUM.*) Don't that little girl look just like Martha Pentecost?

BERTHA. (*Picks up dishpan of dishes and crosses to the pantry.*) I still say he could be talking about anybody.

SETH. The way he described her wasn't no doubt about who he was talking about. Described her right down to her toes.

BERTHA. (*Returns to the kitchen, picks up butter and puts away in icebox.*) What did you tell him?

SETH. I ain't told him nothing. The way the fellow look I wasn't gonna tell him nothing. I don't know what he looking for her for.

BERTHA. (*Rises.*) What else he have to say? (*Picks up SETH's work gloves, claps together over trashcan, puts them back down on the icebox.*)

SETH. I told you he wasn't for no talking. I told him where the outhouse was and to keep that gal off the front porch and out of my garden. He asked if you'd mind setting a hot tub for the gal and that was about the gist of it.

BERTHA. Well, I wouldn't let it worry me if I was you. Comeon get your sleep. (*Picks up SETH's lunchbucket, swishes out with water, puts down on drainboard.*)

BYNUM. He say he looking for Martha and he a deacon in the church?

SETH. That's what he say. Do he look like a deacon to you?

BERTHA. (*Turns to SETH.*) He might be, you don't know. Bynum ain't go no special say on whether he a deacon or not.

SETH. Well, if he the deacon I'd sure like to see the preacher.

(*They all laugh.*)

BERTHA. Comeon get your sleep. Jeremy, don't forget to set them sheets outside the door like I told you.

JEREMY. Yes, ma'am.

(*BERTHA exits into the bedroom.*)

SETH. Something ain't setting right with that fellow, Bynum. He's one of them mean looking niggers look like he done killed somebody gambling over a quarter.

BYNUM. He ain't no gambler. Gamblers wear nice shoes. This fellow got on clodhoppers. He been out there walking up and down them roads.

(*ZONIA enters the kitchen from the stairs and looks around.*)

BYNUM. You looking for the back door, sugar? (*Indicates porch door.*) There it is. You can go out there and play. It's alright.

(*ZONIA crosses hesitantly past SETH.*)

SETH. (*Opens the porch door for her.*) You can go out there and play. Just don't get in my garden. And don't go messing around in my workshed.

(*ZONIA goes out onto the porch and looks out toward the cellar door path. Not finding anyone to play with, she crosses dejectedly to the porch steps and sits. SETH exits into the bedroom. There is a knock on the door. BYNUM sings "They tell me Joe Turner's come and gone. Oh Lordy ...". JEREMY looks toward SETH's bedroom door.*)

JEREMY. (*To BYNUM.*) Somebody at the door.

(*There is another knock on the door. JEREMY goes through the hallway and answers the front door to find MATTIE CAMPBELL. She is a young woman of twenty-six whose attractiveness is hidden under the weight and concerns of a dissatisfied life. She is a woman on an honest search for love and companionship. SHE has suffered many defeats in her search, and though not always uncompromising, still believes in the possibility of love. BYNUM stops singing as MATTIE speaks.)*

MATTIE. I'm looking for a man named Bynum. Lady told me to come back later.

JEREMY. Sure, he here. (*Goes back to the kitchen and stops at the upstage center table.*) Mr. Bynum, somebody here to see you.

(*BYNUM rises, moves up through the arch into the hallway. JEREMY watches MATTIE over his shoulder.*)

BYNUM. Come to see me, huh?

MATTIE. Are you the man they call Bynum? The man folks say can fix things?

BYNUM. Depend on what need fixing. I can't make no promises. But I got a powerful song in some matters.

MATTIE. (*Distraught.*) Can you fix it so my man come back to me?

BYNUM. (*Moves quickly towards her, gestures to the parlor.*) Comeon in ...

(*MATTIE enters, crosses the threshold and into the parlor. BYNUM closes the front door, pulls out the stage right chair.*)

BYNUM. Have a sit down.

MATTIE. (*Sits, as BYNUM moves to the love seat and sits.*) You got to help me. I don't know what else to do.

BYNUM. Depend on all the circumstances of the thing come together. How all the pieces fit.

MATTIE. I done everything I knowed how to do. You got to make him come back to me.

BYNUM. It ain't nothing to make somebody come back. I can fix it so he can't stand to be away from you. I got my roots and powders, I can fix it so wherever he's at this thing will come up on him and he won't be able to sleep for seeing your face. Won't be able to eat for thinking of you.

MATTIE. That's what I want. Make him come back.

(*JEREMY moves to the sliding door, listens.*)

BYNUM. The roots is a powerful thing. I can fix it so one day he'll walk out his front door ... won't be thinking of nothing. He won't know what it is. All he knows is that a powerful dissatisfaction done set in his bones and can't nothing he do make him feel satisfied. He'll set his foot down on the road and the wind in the trees be talking to him and everywhere he step on the road, that road'll give back your name and something will pull him right up to your doorstep. Now, I can do that. I can take my roots and fix that easy. But maybe he ain't supposed to come back ... then he'll be in your bed one morning and it'll come up on him that he's in the wrong place. That he's lost outside of time from his place that he's supposed to be in. Then both of you be lost and trapped outside of life and ain't no way for you to get back into it. Cause you lost from yourselves and where the places come together, where you're supposed to be alive, your heart kicking in your chest with a song worth singing.

MATTIE. (*Decisively.*) Make him come back to me. Make his feet say my name on the road. I don't care what else happens. Make him come back.

BYNUM. What's your man's name?

MATTIE. He go by Jack Carper.

(*JEREMY quietly pulls out the stage left chair at the kitchen table and sits, listens.*)

MATTIE. He was born in Alabama then he come to West Texas and find me and we come here. Been here three years before he left. Say I had a curse prayer on me and he started walking down the road and ain't never come back. Somebody told me, say you can fix things like that.

BYNUM. He just got up one day, set his feet on the road and walked away?

MATTIE. You got to make him come back, mister.

BYNUM. Did he say goodbye?

MATTIE. Ain't said nothing. Just started walking. I could see where he disappeared. Didn't look back. Just keep walking. Can't you fix it so he come back. I ain't got no curse prayer on me. I know I ain't.

BYNUM. What made him say you had a curse prayer on you?

MATTIE. Cause the babies died. Me and Jack has two babies. Two little babies that ain't lived two months before they died. He say it's because somebody curse me not to have babies.

BYNUM. He ain't bound to you if the babies died. Look like somebody trying to keep you from being bound up and he's gone on back to whoever it is cause he's already bound to her. Ain't nothing to be done. Somebody else done got a powerful hand in it and ain't nothing to be done to break it. You got to let him go find where he's supposed to be in the world.

MATTIE. Jack done gone off and you telling me to forget about him. All my life I been looking for somebody to stop and stay with me. I done already got too many things to forget about. I take Jack Carper's hand and it feel so rough and strong. Seem like he's the strongest man in the world the way he hold me. Like he's bigger than the whole world and can't nothing bad get to me. Even when he act mean sometimes he still make everything seem okay with the world. Like there's part of it that belongs just to you. Now you telling me to forget about him?

BYNUM. Jack Carper gone off to where he belong. There's somebody searching for your doorstep right now. Ain't no need you fretting over Jack Carper. Right now he's a strong thought in your mind. But everytime you catch yourself fretting over Jack Carper you push that thought away. You push it out your mind and that thought will get weaker and weaker till you wake up one morning and you won't even be able to call him up on your mind.

(BYNUM rises and crosses to the sliding door. He opens it and JEREMY ducks suddenly, puts his head down on the table as if sleeping. BYNUM crosses into the kitchen. He picks up his basket of weeds and rummages in it, picking up each packet and sniffing it until he finds the right one. He crosses back into the parlor and hands the packet to MATTIE.)

BYNUM. Take this and sleep with in under your pillow and it'll bring good luck to you. Draw it to you like a magnet. It won't be long before you forget all about Jack Carper.

MATTIE. How much do I owe you?

BYNUM. Whatever you got there ... that'll be alright.

(*MATTIE hands BYNUM a quarter.*)

BYNUM. You sleep with that under your pillow and you'll be alright.

(*BYNUM crosses to the stairs and continues halfway up. MATTIE looks at packet, puts it in her purse. She rises, and turns to leave. JEREMY startles her by his presence and engages her in conversation. BYNUM pauses on the stairs to listen.*)

JEREMY. I overheard what you told Mr. Bynum. Had me an old gal did that to me. Woke up one morning and she was gone. Just took off to parts unknown. I woke up that morning and the only thing I could do was look around for my shoes. I woke up and got out of there. Found my shoes and took off. That's the only thing I could think of to do.

MATTIE. She ain't said nothing?

JEREMY. I just looked around for my shoes and got out of there.

MATTIE. Jack ain't said nothing either. He just walked off.

JEREMY. Some mens do that. Womens too. I ain't gone off looking for her. I just let her go. Figure she had a time to come to herself. Wasn't no use of me standing in the way. Where you from?

(*BYNUM exits upstairs with his basket.*)

MATTIE. Texas. I was born in Georgia but I went to Texas with my mama. She dead now. Was picking peaches and fell dead away. I come up here with Jack Carper.

JEREMY. (*Rises, crosses into the parlor.*) I'm from North Carolina. Down around Raleigh where they got all that tobacco. Been up here about two weeks. I likes it fine except I still got to find me a woman. (*Steps closer to MATTIE.*) You got a nice look to you. Look like you have mens standing in your door. Is you got mens standing in your door to get a look at you?

MATTIE. I ain't got nobody since Jack left.

JEREMY. A woman like you need a man. Maybe you let me be your man. I got a nice way with the women. That's what they tell me.

MATTIE. I don't know. Maybe Jack's coming back.

(*MATTIE crosses quickly to the front door. JEREMY pursues her into the hallway.*)

JEREMY. I'll be your man till he come. A woman can't be by her lonesome. Let me be your man till he come.

MATTIE. I just can't go through life piecing myself out to different mens. I need a man who wants to stay with me.

JEREMY. I can't say what's gonna happen. Maybe I'll be that man. I don't know. You wanna go along the road a little way with me.

MATTIE. (*Moves back into the parlor, away from him.*) I don't know. Seem like life say it's gonna be one thing and end up being another. (*Sits in the upstage armchair.*) I'm tired of going from man to man.

JEREMY. (*Persistently. Moves to her.*) Life is like you got to take a chance. Everybody got to take a chance. Can't nobody say what's gonna be. Comeon ... take a chance and be with me and see what the year bring. Maybe you let me come and see you. Where you staying?

MATTIE. I got me a room up on Bedford. Me and Jack had a room together.

JEREMY. What's the address? I'll come by and get you tonight and we can go down to Seefus. I'm going down there and play my guitar.

MATTIE. (*Suddenly brightens.*) You play guitar?

JEREMY. (*Boastfully.*) I play guitar like I'm born to it.

MATTIE. (*Decisively.*) I live at 1727 Bedford Avenue. I'm gonna find out if you can play guitar like you say.

JEREMY. I plays it sugar, and that ain't all I do. I got a ten pound hammer and I knows how to drive it down. Good god ... you ought to hear my hammer ring!

MATTIE. (*Shyly embarrassed. Rises and turns to him.*) Go on with that kind of talk now. If you gonna come by and get me I got to get home and straighten up for you.

JEREMY. I'll be by at eight o'clock. How's eight o'clock?

(*MATTIE nods, moves to the front door, and opens it. JEREMY follows hard at her heels.*)

JEREMY. I'm gonna make you forget all about Jack Carper.

MATTIE. Go on now. I got to get home and fix up for you. (*Exits stage left through the front door.*)
JEREMY. (*Calls out after her.*) Eight o'clock sugar.

(*JEREMY closes the front door, and lets out a whoop as he slaps his cap on his thigh. He exits upstairs as the LIGHTS: fade in the parlor and kitchen and come up on the yard and the porch steps outside.*)

ACT I

Scene 2

ZONIA begins to sing, clapping and slapping her thighs in time to the rhythm, as SOUND: birds chirp intermittently in the back yard. She rises and moves quickly down the path toward the corner of the porch to see what is there.

ZONIA.
I WENT DOWNTOWN
TO GET MY GRIP
I CAME BACK HOME

(*REUBEN enters around the upstage right fence, watches her.*)

ZONIA.
JUST A PULLIN' THE SKIFF
JUST A PULLIN' THE SKIFF

(*ZONIA discovers the flagstones in the path. She hops from stone to stone on her way to the cellar door. REUBEN follows stealthily to the downstage corner of the porch.*)

ZONIA.
I WENT UPSTAIRS
TO MAKE MY BED
I MADE A MISTAKE
AND I BUMPED MY HEAD
JUST A PULLIN' THE SKIFF
JUST A PULLIN' THE SKIFF
I WENT DOWNSTAIRS
TO MILK THE COW
I MADE A MISTAKE
AND I MILKED THE COW

(*ZONIA reaches out and pulls imaginary skiff towards her each time.*)

JUST A PULLIN' THE SKIFF
JUST A PULLIN' THE SKIFF

(*ZONIA arrives at the cellar door. She jumps back and forth, off and on the stage right door. REUBEN follows her unobserved.*)

TOMORROW, TOMORROW
TOMORROW NEVER COMES
THE MORROW, THE MORROW
THE MORROW IN THE BONE.

(*REUBEN runs to the cellar door and leaps across it to the
    stage left side. ZONIA jumps back away from the door
    in surprise.*)

REUBEN. Hi.
ZONIA. Hi.
REUBEN. What's your name?
ZONIA. Zonia.
REUBEN. What kind of name is that?
ZONIA. It's what my daddy named me.
REUBEN. (*Sits on the stage left door.*) My name's
Reuben. You staying in Mr. Seth's house?
ZONIA. Yeah.
REUBEN. That your daddy I seen you with this
morning?
ZONIA. I don't know. Who you seen me with?
REUBEN. I saw you with some man had on a great
big old coat. And you was walking up to Mr. Seth's
house. Had on a hat too.
ZONIA. (*Jumps up on stage right door and sits.*)
Yeah, that's my daddy.
REUBEN. (*Crouches, searches through the rocks in
front of the door for a good one.*) You like Mr. Seth?
ZONIA. I ain't see him much.
REUBEN. (*Sits, places rocks on door next to him.*)
My grandpap say he a great big old windbag. How come
you living in Mr. Seth's house? Don't you have no house?
ZONIA. We going to find my mother.
REUBEN. Where she at?
ZONIA. I don't know. We got to find her. We just go
all over.
REUBEN. Why you got to find her? What happened to
her?

ZONIA. She ran away.

REUBEN. Why she run away?

ZONIA. I don't know. My daddy say some man named Joe Turner did something bad to him once and that made her run away.

REUBEN. Maybe she coming back and you don't have to go looking for her.

ZONIA. We ain't there no more.

REUBEN. She could have come back when you wasn't there.

ZONIA. My daddy said she run off and left us so we going looking for her.

REUBEN. What he gonna do when he find her?

ZONIA. (*Picks through rocks at her feet.*) He didn't say. He just say he got to find her.

REUBEN. You daddy say how long you staying in Mr. Seth's house?

ZONIA. He don't say much. But we never stay too long nowhere. He say we got to keep moving till we find her.

REUBEN. Ain't no kids hardly live around here. I had me a friend but he died. He was the best friend I ever had.

(*Pulls toys and string loop out of his pocket, places toys on the door next to him. Makes a "cup and saucer" figure with the string loop.*)

REUBEN. Me and Eugene used to keep secrets. I still got his pigeons. He told me to let them go when he died. He say, "Reuben, promise me when I die you'll let my pigeons go." But I keep them to remember him by. I ain't never gonna let them go. Even when I get to be grown up. I'm just always gonna have Eugene's pigeons. (*Pauses.*

Shows string figure to ZONIA.) Mr. Bynum a conjure man. My grandpap scared of him. He don't like me to come over here too much. I'm scared of him too. My grandpap told me not to let him get close enough to where he can reach out his hand and touch me.

(*REUBEN reaches out suddenly to touch her, and surprises ZONIA. He moves to put the string loop back in his pocket. ZONIA touches his hand, and stops him. She takes the string from him.*)

ZONIA. He don't seem scary to me. (*Quickly makes a "cup and saucer" figure, and shows it to REUBEN.*)

REUBEN. He buys pigeons from me ... and if you get up early in the morning you can see him out in the yard doing something with them pigeons. My grandpap say he kill them. I sold him one yesterday. I don't know what he do with it. I just hope he don't spook me up.

(*LOOMIS enters from upstairs, in the house. He goes through the kitchen, listening for ZONIA. REUBEN and ZONIA play "cat's cradle," exchanging the string back and forth.*)

ZONIA. Why you sell him pigeons if he's gonna spook you up?

(*LOOMIS crosses to the porch door, opens it and steps out onto the porch, still listening for the direction of their voices.*)

REUBEN. I just do like Eugene do. He used to sell Mr. Bynum pigeons. That's how he got to collecting them to sell to Mr. Bynum. Sometime he give me a nickel and sometime he give me a whole dime.

LOOMIS. (*Comes down the porch stairs to the yard.*) Zonia!

ZONIA. (*Rises quickly, tosses string to REUBEN.*) Sir?

(*LOOMIS crosses down the path to below the porch. He cannot see REUBEN, who is still seated on the cellar door around the corner.*)

LOOMIS. What you doing?

ZONIA. Nothing.

LOOMIS. You stay around this house, you hear? I don't want you wandering off nowhere.

ZONIA. I ain't wandering off nowhere.

LOOMIS. Miss Bertha set that hot tub and you getting a good scrubbing. Get scrubbed up good. You ain't been scrubbing.

ZONIA. I been scrubbing.

LOOMIS. (*Moves in to ZONIA.*) Look at you. You growing too fast. Your bones getting bigger everyday. I don't want you getting grown on me. Don't you get grown on me too soon. We gonna find your mama. (*LOOMIS looks out to yard.*) She around here somewhere. I can smell her.

(*REUBEN peeks out from corner to see LOOMIS. LOOMIS turns back to ZONIA, spies REUBEN. REUBEN ducks back around the corner. LOOMIS crosses around ZONIA to the cellar door. His eyes*

*meet REUBEN's. LOOMIS looks at him pointedly.
He turns to ZONIA.)*

LOOMIS. You stay around this house now. Don't you
go nowhere.
ZONIA. Yes, sir.

*(LOOMIS smoothes ZONIA's hair back from her forehead,
and exits into the house through the porch door,
continues through the hallway and out the front door.
ZONIA sits back down on the stage right door.)*

REUBEN. *(Puts his toys away in his pocket.)* Wow,
your daddy's scary!
ZONIA. He is not! I don't know what you talking
about.
REUBEN. He got them mean looking eyes!
ZONIA. *(Rises, walks rapidly away from the cellar
door.)* My daddy ain't go no mean looking eyes!
REUBEN. *(Rises, jumps off the cellar door and runs
to catch up with ZONIA.)* Aw. girl, I was just messing
with you.

(ZONIA stops walking away, and turns back to REUBEN.)

REUBEN. You wanna go see Eugene's pigeons? Got a
great big coop out the back of my house. Comeon, I'll
show you.

*(REUBEN runs around ZONIA to exit offstage upstage
right. ZONIA hesitates, looks back to cellar door,
turns and runs after him to exit as the LIGHTS: fade to
black and SOUND: music fades up.)*

ACT I

Scene 3

It is Saturday morning, one week later. LIGHTS: fade up on the kitchen as SOUND: music fades out. BERTHA is at the stove putting a pan of biscuits in the oven, while SETH sits stage right of the kitchen table, repairing a broom.

SETH. Something ain't right about that fellow. I been watching him all week. Something ain't right I'm telling you.

BERTHA. (*Picks up excess dough, wraps in cloth, puts in icebox.*) Seth Holly, why don't you hush up about that man this morning. (*Picks up the lunch pail, rinses out it the sink, puts down on the drainboard.*)

SETH. I don't like the way he stares at everybody. Don't look at you natural like. He just be staring at you. Like he trying to figure out something about you. Did you see him when he come back in here?

BERTHA. (*Picks up the salt and pepper shakers and sugar bowl, puts them on the stove shelf.*) That man ain't thinking about you.

SETH. He don't work nowhere. Just go out and come back. Go out and come back.

BERTHA. As long as you get your boarding money it ain't your cause about what he do. He don't bother nobody. (*Goes into the pantry, picks up her mending basket.*)

SETH. Just go out and come back. Going around asking everybody about Martha. Like Henry Allen seen him down at the church last night.

BERTHA. (*Comes back into the kitchen, puts the basket down on the stage left end of the kitchen table.*) The man's allowed to go to church if he want. He say he a deacon. Ain't nothing wrong about him going to church.

SETH. I ain't talking about him going to church. I'm talking about him hanging around *outside* the church.

BERTHA. Henry Allen say that?

SETH. Say he be standing around outside the church. Like he be watching it.

BERTHA. (*Sits in the stage left chair, picks up a sock, puts the wooden egg in, begins to darn the hole.*) What on earth he wanna be watching the church for I wonder?

SETH. That's what I'm trying to figure out. Looks like he fixing to rob it.

BERTHA. Seth, now do he look like the kind that would rob the church?

SETH. I ain't saying that. I ain't saying how he look. It's how he do. Anybody liable to do anything as far as I'm concerned. I ain't never thought about how no church robbers look ... but now that you mention it, I don't see where they look no different than how he look.

BERTHA. Herald Loomis ain't the kind of man who would rob no church.

SETH. I ain't even so sure that's his name.

BERTHA. Why the man got to lie about his name?

SETH. Anybody can tell anybody anything about what their name is. That's what you call him ... Herald Loomis. His name is liable to be anything.

BERTHA. Well, until he tell me different that's what I'm gonna call him. You just getting yourself all worked up about the man for nothing.

SETH. Talking about Loomis. Martha's name wasn't no Loomis anything. Martha's name is Pentecost.

BERTHA. How you so sure that's her right name. Maybe she changed it.

SETH. Martha's a good Christian woman. This fellow here look like he owe the devil a day's work and he's trying to figure out how he gonna pay him. Martha ain't had a speck of distrust about her the whole time she was living here. They moved the church out there to Rankin and I was sorry to see her go.

BERTHA. (*Suddenly sees the answer.*) That's why he be hanging around the church. He looking for her.

SETH. If he looking for her, why don't he go inside and ask. What he doing hanging around outside the church acting sneakly like.

(*BYNUM enters from the yard, crosses quickly through the kitchen. SETH stops working on the broom; BERTHA stops mending.*)

BYNUM. (*Continues through the kitchen to the hallway.*) Morning, Seth. Morning, Sister Bertha.

(*BYNUM exits upstairs.*)

BERTHA. That's who you should be asking the questions. He was out there before the sun come up. He didn't even come in for breakfast. I don't know what he's doing. He had three of them pigeons line up out there. (*Demonstrates dance with flapping bird arms.*) He dance around till he get tired. He sit down awhile then get up and dance some more. (*Demonstrates dance with flapping bird arms again.*) He come through here a little while ago looking like he was mad at the world.

(*SETH resumes repairing broom, BERTHA goes back to her mending.*)

SETH. I don't pay Bynum no mind. He don't spook me up with all that stuff.

BERTHA. That's how Martha come to be living here. She come to see Bynum. She come to see him when she first left from down South.

SETH. (*Argumentatively.*) Martha was living here before Bynum. She ain't come on here when she first left from down there. She come on here after she went back to get her little girl. That's when she come on here.

BERTHA. Well, where was Bynum? He was here when she came.

SETH. Bynum ain't come till after her. That boy Hiram was staying up there in Bynum's room.

BERTHA. Well, how long Bynum been here?

SETH. Bynum ain't been here no longer than three years. That's what I'm trying to tell you. Martha was staying up there and sewing and cleaning for Doc Goldblum when Bynum came. This the longest he ever been in one place.

BERTHA. How you know how long the man been in one place?

SETH. I know Bynum. Bynum ain't no mystery to me. I done seen a hundred niggers like him. He's one of them fellows never could stay in one place. He was wandering all around the country till he got old and settled here. The only thing different about Bynum is he bring all this heebie-jeebie stuff with him.

BERTHA. I still say he was staying here when she came. That's why she came ... to see him.

SETH. You can say what you want. I know the facts of it. She come on here four years ago all heart broken cause she couldn't find her little girl. And Bynum wasn't nowhere around. She got mixed up in that old heebie-jeebie nonsense with him after he came.

BERTHA. Well, if she came on before Bynum I don't know where she stayed. Cause she stayed up there in Hiram's room. Hiram couldn't get along with Bynum and left out of here owing you two dollars. Now I know you ain't forgot about that!

SETH. (*Pauses, considering, suddenly remembers.*) Sure did!

(*BERTHA suddenly remembers the biscuits in the oven, rises quickly, moves to the stove, takes them out and places them on the downstage left burner.*)

SETH. You know Hiram ain't payed me that two dollars yet. So that's why he be ducking and hiding when he see me down on Logan Street. You right. Martha did come on after Bynum. I forgot that's why Hiram left.

BERTHA. (*Crosses back to the kitchen table near SETH.*) Him and Bynum could never see eye to eye. They always rubbed each other the wrong way. Hiram got to thinking that Bynum was trying to put a fix on him and he moved out. Martha came to see Bynum and ended up taking Hiram's room. Now I know that I'm talking about. She stayed on here three years till they moved the church. (*Goes *to the mending basket and takes the egg out of the sock, puts both back in the basket.)*

SETH. She out there in Rankin now.

(BERTHA looks at SETH in surprise.)

SETH. I know where she at. I know where they moved the church to. She right out there in Rankin in that place used to be shoe store. Used to be Wolfe's shoe store. They moved to a bigger place and they put that church in there. I know just where she at.

BERTHA. Why don't you tell the man? You see he looking for her.

SETH. I ain't gonna tell that man where that woman is! What I wanna do that for? I don't know nothing about that man. I don't know why he looking for her. He might wanna do her a harm.

(BERTHA, disbelieving, picks up the mending basket and puts it back in the pantry.)

SETH. I ain't gonna carry that on my hands. He looking for her, he gonna have to find her for himself. I ain't gonna help him. Now if he had come and presented himself as a gentleman ... the way Martha Pentecost's husband would have done ... then I would have told him.

(BERTHA comes back into kitchen, goes to SETH.)

SETH. But I ain't gonna tell this old wild-eyed mean looking nigger nothing!

BERTHA. Well, why don't you get a ride with Selig and go up there and tell her where he is. See if she wanna see him. If that's her little girl ... you say Martha was looking for her.

SETH. You know me, Bertha. I don't get mixed up in nobody's business.

(*BYNUM enters from the stairs, puts his basket down in the upstage left corner of the kitchen on the floor. BERTHA moves to the stove.*)

BYNUM. (*Rises, crosses to his chair.*) Morning, Seth. Morning, Sister Bertha. Can I still get some breakfast?

(*BERTHA nods, resigned, picks up a place setting from the upstage center table as BYNUM sits in the upstage right chair.*)

BYNUM. Mr. Loomis been down here this morning?

(*BERTHA puts the place setting in front of BYNUM, fixes a plate with a biscuit, dishes up a bowl of grits and leaves them on the stove.*)

SETH. He done gone out and come back. He up there now. Left out of here early this morning wearing that coat. Hot as it is the man wanna walk around wearing a big old heavy coat. He come back in here paid me for another week, sat down there waiting for Selig. Got tired of waiting and went on back upstairs.

BYNUM. Where's the little girl?

SETH. She out there in the front. Had to chase her and that Reuben off the front porch. She out there somewhere.

BYNUM. Look like if Martha was around here he would have found her by now. My guess is she ain't in the city.

(*BERTHA picks up the coffee pot, moves down to BYNUM, pours his coffee.*)

SETH. She ain't! I know where she at. I know just where she at. But I ain't gonna tell him. Not the way he look.

BERTHA. (*Places cup in front of him.*) Here go your coffee, Bynum. (*Goes to the stove, puts the coffee pot down, and picks up the plate with the biscuit.*)

BYNUM. He say he gonna get Selig to find her for him.

SETH. Selig can't find her. He talk all that ... but unless he get lucky and knock on her door he can't find her. That's the only way he find anybody. He got to get lucky. But I know just where she at.

BERTHA. (*Puts place in front of BYNUM.*) Here go your biscuit, Bynum.

(*BERTHA goes back to the stove and picks up the bowl of grits, hides them behind her back and comes back to BYNUM.*)

BYNUM. What else you got over there, Sister Bertha? You got some grits and gravy over there?

(*BERTHA sets the bowl on the table. Relishing it.*)

BYNUM. I could go for some of that this morning.

BERTHA. (*Crosses to the archway.*) Seth, comeon and help me turn this mattress over. (*Turns back to see he's not following.*) Comeon. (*Exits through the hallway and up the stairs.*)

SETH. (*Rises with the broom, places it in the fireplace, stage left of the stove.*) Something ain't right with that fellow, Bynum. I don't like the way he stare at everybody.

BYNUM. Mr. Loomis alright, Seth. He just a man got something on his mind. He just got a straightforward mind, that's all.

SETH. What's that fellow they had around here? Moses? That's Moses Houser. Man went crazy and jumped off the Brady Street Bridge. I told you when I seen him something wasn't right about him. And I'm telling you about this fellow now.

(*There is a KNOCK on the porch door. SETH goes to answer it, opens the door. Enter RUTHERFORD SELIG.*)

SETH. Ho! Comeon in, Selig.

BYNUM. If it ain't the People Finder himself.

SETH. (*Cuts him off.*) Bynum, before you start ... I ain't seen no shiny man now. (*Takes his money out of the shoulder bag and turns to SETH.*)

BYNUM. (*Chuckles to himself.*) Who said anything about that. I ain't said nothing about that. I just called you a First Class People Finder.

SELIG. How many dustpans you get out of that sheet metal, Seth?

SETH. You walked by them on your way in. They sitting out there by the shed. Got twenty-eight. Got four out of each sheet and made Bertha a coffee pot out the other one. They a little small but they got nice handles.

SELIG. That was twenty cents apiece, right? That's what we agreed on.

SETH. (*Rapidly.*) That's five dollars and sixty cents. Twenty on top of twenty-eight. How many sheets you bring me?

SELIG. I got eight out there. That's a dollar twenty makes me owe you ...

SETH. (*Even faster.*) Four dollars and forty cents.

SELIG. (*Pays him.*) Go on and make me some more dustpans. I can use all you can make.

(*LOOMIS enters from the stairs, moves down into the kitchen next to BYNUM*)

LOOMIS. I been watching you. He say you find people.

BYNUM. Mr. Loomis here wants you to find his wife.

LOOMIS. He say you find people. Find her for me.

SELIG. (*Sits in the upstage right chair.*) Well, let me see here ... find somebody is it?

(*SELIG rummages around through his pockets. He has several notebooks and he is searching for the right one. He finds it, opens, and preparing to write, licks his pencil.*)

SELIG. Alright now ... what's the name?

LOOMIS. Martha Loomis. She my wife. Got married legal with the paper and all.

SELIG. (*Writes slowly.*) Martha ... Loomis. How tall is she?

LOOMIS. She five feet from the ground.

SETH. (*Writes.*) Five feet ... tall. Young or old?

LOOMIS. She a young woman. Got long pretty hair.

SETH. (*Writes slowly.*) Young ... long ... pretty ... hair. Where did you last see her?

LOOMIS. Tennessee. Nearby Memphis.

SELIG. When was that?

LOOMIS. Nineteen hundred and one.

SELIG. (*Writes.*) Nineteen ... hundred and one. (*Pockets notebooks and pencil.*) I'll tell you mister ... you better off without them. Now you take me ... old Rutherford Selig could tell you a thing or two about these women. I ain't met one yet I could understand. Now you take Sally out there. That's all a man need is a good horse. I say giddup and she go. Say, whoa and she stop. I feed her some oats and she carry me wherever I want to go. Ain't had a speck of trouble out of her since I had her. Now I been married. A long time ago down in Kentucky. I got up one morning and I saw this look on my wife's face. Like way down deep inside her she was wishing I was dead. I walked around that morning and every time I looked at her she had that look on her face. It seem like she knew I could see it on her. Everytime I looked at her I got smaller and smaller. Well, I wasn't gonna stay around there and just shrink away. I walked out on the porch and closed the door behind me. When I closed the door she locked it. I went out and bought me a horse. Ain't been without one since.

(*SELIG, SETH and BYNUM share a good laugh. They cut it short when they notice LOOMIS is not laughing.*)

SELIG. Martha Loomis, huh? Well, now I'll do the best I can do. That's one dollar.

LOOMIS. (*Suspiciously.*) How you find her?

SELIG. Well, now it ain't no easy job like you think. You can't just go out here and find them like that. There's a lot of little tricks to it. It's not an easy job keeping up with you nigras the way you move about so. Now you take this woman you looking for ... this Martha Loomis. She could be anywhere. Time I find her, if you don't keep your eye on her, she'll be gone off someplace else. You'll be thinking she over here and she'll be over there. But like I say there's a lot of little tricks to it.

LOOMIS. (*Accusingly.*) You say you find her.

SELIG. I can't promise anything but we been finders in my family for a long time. Bringers and finders. My great-grand-daddy used to bring nigras across the ocean on ships. That wasn't no easy job either. Sometimes the winds would blow so hard you'd think the hand of God was set against the sails. But it set him well and pay and he settled in this new land and found him a wife of good Christian charity with a mind for kids and the like and well ... here I am, Rutherford Selig. You're in good hands, mister. Me and my daddy have found plenty nigras. My daddy, rest his soul, used to find runaway slaves for the plantation bosses. He was the best there was at it. Jonas B. Selig. Had him a reputation stretched clean across the country. After Abraham Lincoln give you all nigras your freedom papers and with you all looking all over for each other ... we started finding nigras for nigras.

(*LOOMIS, decided, reaches in his pocket for his last dollar.*)

SELIG. Of course, it don't pay as much. But the People Finding business ain't so bad.

LOOMIS. (*Moves above BYNUM and holds the dollar out to SELIG.*) Find her.

(*SELIG reaches for dollar bill. LOOMIS keeps hold of it and meets his eyes.*)

LOOMIS. Martha Loomis. Find her for me. (*Releases dollar to SELIG.*)
SELIG. Like I say, I can't promise you anything. I'm going back up river, and if she's around in them parts I'll find her for you. But I can't promise you anything. (*Turns to go, stops as LOOMIS speaks.*)
LOOMIS. When you coming back?
SELIG. (*Turns to LOOMIS.*) I'll be back on Saturday. I come and see Seth to pick up my order on Saturday.
BYNUM. You going upriver, huh? You going up around my way. I used to go all up through there. Blawknox, Claiton.

(*SELIG takes another step to the porch door. Insistently.*)

BYNUM. Used to go up to Rankin and take that first right hand road.

(*SETH looks pointedly at BYNUM.*)

BYNUM. I wore many a pair of shoes out walking around that way. You'd have thought I was a missionary spreading the gospel the way I wandered all around them parts.

SELIG. (*Cuts him off, crosses to the porch door.*)
Okay, Bynum. See you on Saturday.

SETH. (*Follows SELIG.*) Here, let me walk out with
you. Help you with them dustpans.

(*SETH and SELIG exit out the back. BERTHA enters
    from the stairs carrying a pillowcase full of sheets,
    stops in the pantry and picks up a washboard. She
    comes into the kitchen.*)

BYNUM. Herald Loomis got the People Finder
looking for his wife.

BERTHA. (*Crosses to the icebox, puts down the
washboard on top, pulls the washtub out from under the
sink.*) You can call him a People Finder if you want to. I
know Rutherford Selig carries people away too. He done
carried a whole bunch of them away from here. Folks plan
on leaving plan by Selig's timing. (*Rises, turns to
LOOMIS.*) They wait till he get ready to go then they
hitch a ride on his wagon. Then he charge folks a dollar to
tell them where he took them. (*Turns back to the sink and
drops the sheets in the tub. Picks up the soap.*) Now that's
the truth of Rutherford Selig. This old People Finding
business is for the birds. He ain't never found nobody he
ain't took away. (*Turns to LOOMIS.*) Herald Loomis you
just wasted your dollar.

LOOMIS. He say he find her. He say he find her by
Saturday. I'm gonna wait till Saturday.

(*LOOMIS turns and exits up the stairs, and BERTHA
    bends down over her washing as the LIGHTS: fade to
    black and SOUND: music fades up.*)

ACT I

Scene 4

It is Sunday morning, the next day. The LIGHTS: fade up on the kitchen as the SOUND: music fades out. SETH stands next to sink, looks in mirror, shaves, as he talks to BYNUM, who is still seated at his place upstage left. The breakfast dishes have been cleared away. BYNUM is sewing an herb packet, his weed basket is on the table in front of him. The sliding door is open.

SETH. (*His favorite topic.*) They can't see that. Neither one of them can see that. Now how much sense it take to see that? All you got to do is be able to count. One man making ten pots is five men making fifty pots. But they can't see that. Asked where I'm gonna get my five men. Hell, I can teach anybody how to make a pot. I can teach you. I can take you out there and get you started right now. Inside of two weeks you'd know how to make a pot. All you got to do is want to do it. I can get five men. I ain't worried about getting no five men.

BERTHA. (*Opens bedroom door, sticks her head out. She is changing clothes for church.*) Seth. Comeon and get ready now. Reverend Gates ain't gonna be holding up his sermon cause you sitting out there talking.

SETH. (*Stops shaving, turns to BYNUM.*) Now you take the boy, Jeremy. What he gonna do after he put in that road? He can't do nothing but go put in another one somewhere. Now if he let me show him how to make some pots and pans ... then he'd have something can't nobody take away from him. After awhile he could get his own tools and go off somewhere and make his own pots and pans. Find him somebody to sell them to. Now Selig can't make no pots and pans. He can sell them but he can't make them. I get me five men with some tools and we'd make him so many pots and pans he'd have to open up a store somewhere. But they can't see that. Neither Mr. Johnson nor Sam Green.

BERTHA. (*Calls from the bedroom.*) Seth ... time be wasting. Best be getting on.

SETH. I'm coming woman! (*To BYNUM.*) Want me to sign over the house to borrow five hundred dollars. I ain't that big a fool. That's all I got. Sign it over to them and then I won't have nothing.

(*SETH wipes the excess shaving soap off his face with the towel over his shoulder and checks himself in the mirror as JEREMY enters from the front door, moves through the parlor to the stage left end of the kitchen table, waving a dollar and carrying his guitar.*)

JEREMY. Look here, Mr. Bynum ... won me another dollar last night down at Seefus! (*Slams the dollar down on the table.*) Me and that Mattie Campbell went down there again and I played contest. Say, Mr. Seth, (*Picks up the dollar, leans the guitar against the upstage center table, and goes to SETH.*) I asked Mattie Campbell if she wanna come by and have Sunday dinner with us. Get some fried chicken.

SETH. It's gonna cost you twenty-five cents.

JEREMY. That's alright. I got a whole dollar here. (*Removes his cap and holds it front of him. Shyly.*) Say, Mr. Seth ... me and Mattie Campbell talked it over last night and she gonna move in with me. If that's alright with you.

SETH. (*Turns to JEREMY.*) Your business is your business ... but it's gonna cost her a dollar a week for her board. I can't be feeding nobody for free. (*Picks up the shaving mug, brush, and razor in one hand.*)

JEREMY. (*Holds dollar out to SETH.*) Oh, she know that, Mr. Seth. That's what I told her, say she'd have to pay for her meals. (*Reaches in his pocket and holds out some change.*) You say you got a whole dollar there ... turn loose that twenty-five cents.

JEREMY. (*Snatches dollar back. Bargains.*) Suppose she move in today then that make seventy-five cents more, so I'll give you the whole dollar for her now till she gets here.

(*SETH hesitates, grabs the dollar bill, pockets the money, and exits into the bedroom. JEREMY lets out a whoop, and slaps his thigh with his cap.*)

BYNUM. So you and that Mattie Campbell gonna take up together?

JEREMY. (*Hangs his cap on SETH's chair, stage right.*) I told her she don't need to be by her lonesome, Mr. Bynum. Don't make no sense for both of us to be by our lonesome. So she gonna move in with me. (*Sits in SETH's chair.*)

BYNUM. Sometimes you got to be where you supposed to be. Sometimes you can get all mixed up in life and come to the wrong place.

JEREMY. That's just what I told her, Mr. Bynum. It don't make no sense for her to be all mixed up and lonesome. May as well come here and be with me. She a fine woman too. Got them long legs. Knows how to treat a fellow too. Treat you like you wanna be treated.

BYNUM. (*Puts down his sewing.*) You just can't look at it like that. You got to look at the whole thing. Now you take a fellow go out there, grab hold to a woman and think he got something cause she sweet and soft to the touch.. Alright. Touching's a part of life. It's in the world like everything else. Touching's nice. It feels good. But you can lay you hand upside a horse or a cat, and that feels good too. What's the difference? When you grab hold to a woman, you got you something there. You got a whole world there. You got a way of life kicking up under your hand. That woman can take and make you feel like something. I ain't just talking about in the way of jumping off into bed together and rolling around with each other. Anybody can do that. When you grab hold to that woman and look at the whole thing and see what you got ... why she can take and make something out of you. Your mother was a woman. That's enough right there to show you what a woman is. Enough to show you what she can do. She made something out of you. Taught you converse, and all about how to take care of yourself, how to see where you at and where you going tomorrow, how to look out to see what's coming in the way of eating, and what to do with yourself when you get lonesome. That's a mighty thing she did. But you just can't look at a woman to jump off into bed with her. That's a foolish thing to ignore a woman like that.

JEREMY. Oh, I ain't ignoring her, Mr. Bynum. It's hard to ignore a woman got legs like she got.

BYNUM. (*Laughs.*) Alright. Let's try it this way. Now you take a ship. Be out there on the water traveling about. You out there on the ship sailing to and from. And then you see some land. Just like you see a woman walking down the street. You see that land and it don't look like nothing but a line out there on the horizon. That's all it is when you first see it. A line that cross your path out there on the horizon. Now, a smart man know when he see that land, it ain't just a line setting out there. He know that if you get off the water to go take a good look ... why there's a whole world right there. A whole world with everything imaginable under the sun. Anything you can think of you can find on that land. Same with a woman. A woman is everything a man need. That's all he need to live on. You give me some water and berries and if there ain't nothing else I can live a hundred years. (*JEREMY tries to interrupt. BYNUM cuts him off.*) See, you just like a man looking at the horizon from a ship. You just seeing a part of it. But it's a blessing when you learn to look at a woman and see in maybe just a few strands of her hair, the way her cheek curves ... to see in that everything there is out of life to be gotten. It's a blessing to see that. You know you done right and proud by your mother to see that. But you got to learn it. My telling you ain't gonna mean nothing. You got to learn how to come to your own time and place with a woman.

JEREMY. What about your woman, Mr. Bynum. I know you done had some women.

BYNUM. Oh, I got them in memory time. That lasts longer than any of them ever stayed with me.

JEREMY. I had me an old gal one time ...

(*There is a knock on the front door. JEREMY hesitates and looks to the bedroom for SETH. BYNUM sings "They tell me Joe Turner's come and gone ..." There is a second knock, more persistent. JEREMY goes to answer it. He opens the front door, and steps back in awe. Enter MOLLY CUNNINGHAM. She is about twenty-six, the kind that "could break in on a dollar anywhere she goes." She carries a small cardboard suitcase, and wears a colorful dress of the fashion of the day. JEREMY's heart jumps out of his chest when he sees her.*)

MOLLY. You got any rooms here. I'm looking for a room.
JEREMY. (*Excitedly.*) Yeah ... Mr. Seth got rooms.

(*Gestures toward the parlor. MOLLY moves into the parlor next to the stage right chair. JEREMY closes the front door quickly and moves to stage right of MOLLY.*)

JEREMY. Sure ... wait till I get Mr. Seth. (*Crosses into the kitchen and calls out towards the bedroom.*) Mr. Seth! Somebody here to see you! (*Crosses back to MOLLY.*) Yeah, Mr. Seth got some rooms. Got one right next to me. This is a nice place to stay too. My name's Jeremy. What's yours?

(*JEREMY holds out his hand to shake. MOLLY ignores it, looking around the room. SETH enters dressed in his Sunday clothes.*)

SETH. Ho!

JEREMY. (*Moves up to the kitchen arch to allow room for SETH.*) This here woman looking for a place to stay. She say you got any rooms.

MOLLY. Mister, you got any rooms. I seen your sign say you got rooms.

SETH. (*Moves to MOLLY. Pleasantly.*) How long you plan to staying?

(*JEREMY crosses to below the stove to get a better view of MOLLY.*)

MOLLY. (*Puts her suitcase down on the floor.*) I ain't gonna be here long. I ain't looking for no home or nothing. I'd be in Cincinnati if I hadn't missed my train.

SETH. Rooms cost two dollars a week.

MOLLY. (*Shocked.*) Two dollars!

SETH. (*Reassuring.*) That includes meals. We serve two meals a day. That's breakfast and dinner.

MOLLY. I hope it ain't on the third floor.

SETH. That's the only one I got. Third floor to the left. That's pay up in advance week to week.

(*MOLLY reaches into her bosom for a roll of bills, pulls off two dollars. SETH looks away.*)

MOLLY. I'm gonna pay you for one week. My name's Molly. Molly Cunningham. (*Replaces the roll of bills in her bosom.*)

SETH. I'm Seth Holly. My wife's name is Bertha. She do the cooking and taking care of around here. She got sheets on the bed. Towels twenty-five cents a week extra if you ain't got none. You get breakfast and dinner. We got fried chicken on Sundays.

(*MOLLY takes a change purse out of her handbag, opens it, and extracts one quarter. She replaces the change purse in the handbag.*)

MOLLY. That sounds good. Here's two dollars and twenty-five cents.

(*SETH holds his hand out for the money. MOLLY places it in his palm, leaving her hand in his.*)

MOLLY. Look here, Mister ...?
SETH. Holly. Seth Holly.
MOLLY. (*Withdraws her hand.*) Look here, Mr. Holly, I forgot to tell you. I likes me some company from time to time. I don't like being by myself.
SETH. Your business is your business. I don't meddle in nobody's business. But there is a respectable house. I don't have no riff-raff around here. And I don't have no women hauling no men up to their rooms to be making their living. As long as we understand each other then we'll be alright with each other.
MOLLY. (*Cuts him off.*) Where's the outhouse?
SETH. (*Points to the back door.*) Straight through that door over yonder.
MOLLY. (*Crosses past him, then turns back.*) And I get my own key to the front door?
SETH. (*Easily.*) Everybody get their own key. If you come in late just don't be making no whole lot of noise and carrying on. Don't allow no fussing and fighting around here.
MOLLY. (*Pointedly.*) You ain't got to worry about that, mister. Which way you say that outhouse was again.

SETH. (*Points to the back door again.*) Straight through that door over yonder.

(*MOLLY exits regally through the porch door, passing JEREMY, who inhales her perfume deeply as she goes by. JEREMY moves to the kitchen window and watches her cross the yard as SETH goes to the parlor window and takes down the Rooms-to-Let sign. SETH crosses back to the kitchen and places the sign on the mantel.*)

JEREMY. Mr. Bynum, you know what? (*JEREMY turns to BYNUM.*) I think I know what you was talking about now.

(*JEREMY and BYNUM laugh as the LIGHTS: fade to black and SOUND: music fades up.*)

ACT I

Scene 5

Laughter in the dark. LIGHTS: up in the kitchen as the SOUND: music fades out. It is later that same evening. The gas lamps are lit. MATTIE and all the residents of the house, except LOOMIS, sit around the table. They have finished eating and most of the dishes have been cleared. BYNUM is asleep in his chair. BERTHA stands next to MOLLY. As the laughter subsides, she picks up the chicken platter. MOLLY stops her with a hand to her arm. MOLLY takes the last little bit of chicken off the platter and pops it into her mouth. Everyone laughs as BERTHA puts the platter on the drainboard.

MOLLY. That sure was good chicken.

JEREMY. That's what I'm talking about. Miss Bertha, you sure can fry some chicken. I thought my mama could fry some chicken. But she can't do half as good as you.

SETH. I know it. That's why I married her. She don't know that though. She think I married her for something else.

BERTHA. (*Playfully snaps SETH with the dish towel.*) I ain't studying you Seth. Did you get your things moved in alright Mattie?

MATTIE. I ain't had that much. Jeremy helped me with what I did have.

BERTHA. You'll get to know your way around here. If you have any questions about anything just ask me. You and Molly both. I get along with everybody. You'll find I ain't no trouble to get along with.

MATTIE. (*Reaches for the serving bowl.*) You need some help with the dishes?

BERTHA. (*Takes the bowl from MATTIE.*) I got me a helper. Ain't I Zonia? Got me a good helper.

ZONIA. Yes, ma'am.

(*BERTHA takes the bowl to the sink. MATTIE hands two glasses to ZONIA , who puts them on the drainboard. ZONIA scrapes the bowl and platter into the garbage can. BERTHA begins to wash the glasses.*)

SETH. Look at Bynum sitting over there with his belly all poked out. Ain't saying nothing. Sitting over there half asleep. Ho, Bynum!

BERTHA. (*Turns to SETH.*) If Bynum ain't saying nothing what you wanna start him up for?

SETH. (*Rises and crosses to BYNUM. Shouts in his ear.*) Ho, Bynum!

(*SETH laughs as BYNUM, startled, awakens.*)

BYNUM. What you hollering at me for? I ain't doing nothing.

SETH. Comeon, we gonna Juba.

BYNUM. You know me, I'm always ready to Juba.

SETH. Well, come on then. Comeon there, Jeremy. Where's your guitar. Go get your guitar. Bynum say he's ready to Juba.

JEREMY. Don't need no guitar to Juba. Ain't you never Juba without a guitar?

SETH. (*Starts to hambone.*) It ain't that. I ain't never Juba with one! Figure to try it and see how it worked.

BYNUM. You don't need no guitar. Look at Molly sitting over there. She don't know we Juba on Sunday. We gonna show you something tonight. You and Mattie Campbell both. Ain't that right, Seth?

SETH. You said it! Comeon, Bertha leave them dishes be for awhile. We gonna Juba.

BYNUM. Alright. Let's Juba down.

(*BYNUM starts to drum slowly on the table, picks up momentum and volume as the Juba continues. BERTHA starts to dance around the table with the kitchen towel held aloft. She gestures for MATTIE and*

MOLLY to join in as she passes them. JEREMY also jumps up after MOLLY passes him. MATTIE encourages ZONIA to join, teaching her the steps. The Juba is reminiscent of the Ring Shouts of the African slaves. It is a call and response dance. BYNUM sits at the table and drums. He calls the dance as the others clap hands, shuffle and stomp around the table. SETH takes over the calls as the Juba becomes more impassioned. JEREMY joins in with the drumming at the table. The Juba should be as African as possible, with the performers working themselves up into a near frenzy. The words can be improvised, but should include some mention of the Holy Ghost. At the height of the dance HERALD LOOMIS enters.)

LOOMIS. (*Slams his fist with his hat on the table in a rage.*) Stop it! Stop it! Stop! (*The others stop the dance and respond as if he's preaching to them.*) You all sitting up here singing about the Holy Ghost. What's so Holy about the Holy Ghost? You singing and singing. You think the Holy Ghost coming? You singing for the Holy Ghost to come? What he gonna do, huh? (*They echo him.*) He gonna come with tongues of fire to burn up your wooly heads? (*They stop the response, turn to look at him.*) You gonna tie onto the Holy Ghost and get burned up? What you got then? Why God got to be so big? Why he got to be bigger than me? How much big is there? How much big do you want? (*Starts to unbutton his pants.*)
    SETH. Nigger, you crazy!
    LOOMIS. How much big you want?
    SETH. You done plumb lost your mind!

(*SETH moves toward LOOMIS, who suddenly convulses, begins to speak in tongues and dances rapidly around the kitchen twice. SETH starts after him.*)

BERTHA. Leave him alone, Seth. He ain't in his right mind.

(*Everyone ducks and retreats out of LOOMIS' way. MATTIE holds ZONIA, covering her eyes.*)

LOOMIS. (*Stops suddenly at center stage. Looks at them.*) You all don't know nothing about me. You don't know what I done seen. Herald Loomis done seen some things he ain't got words to tell you.

(*LOOMIS picks up his hat from the table and turns to go. He falls back downstage center as if hit by an incredible force. BYNUM rushes to him. ZONIA starts for him, but MATTIE holds her back. The others watch in fascinated horror.*)

BYNUM. What you done seen, Herald Loomis?
LOOMIS. (*Flat on his back.*) I done seen bones rise up out the water. Rise up and walk across the water. Bones walking on top of the water.
BYNUM. (*Bends over him.*) Tell me about them bones, Herald Loomis. Tell me what you seen.
LOOMIS. (*Kneels, cowering, terror-struck by his vision.*) I come to this place ... to this water that was bigger than the whole world. And I looked out ...(*Rises, still kneeling, looks out and reaches for vision downstage. BYNUM looks out.*) and I seen these bones rise up out the water. Rise up and begin to walk on top of it.

BYNUM. Wasn't nothing but bones and they walking on top of the water.

LOOMIS. Walking without sinking down. Walking on top of the water.

BYNUM. Just marching in a line.

LOOMIS. A whole heap of them. They come up out the water and started marching.

BYNUM. Wasn't nothing but bones and they walking on top of the water.

LOOMIS. One after the other. They just come up out the water and start to walking.

BYNUM. They walking on the water without sinking down. They just walking and walking. And then ... what happened, Herald Loomis?

LOOMIS. They just walking across the water.

BYNUM. What happened, Herald Loomis? What happened to the bones?

LOOMIS. They just walking across the water ... and then ... they sunk down.

BYNUM. The bones sunk into the water. They all sunk down.

LOOMIS. All at one time! They just all fell in the water at one time.

BYNUM. Sunk down like anybody else.

LOOMIS. When they sink down they made a big splash and this here wave come up ...

BYNUM. A big wave, Herald Loomis. A big wave washed over the land.

LOOMIS. It washed them out of the water and up on the land. Only ... only ...

BYNUM. Only they ain't bones no more.

LOOMIS. They got flesh on them! Just like you and me!

BYNUM. Everywhere you look the waves is washing them up on the land right on top of one another.

LOOMIS. They black. Just like you and me. Ain't no difference.

BYNUM. Then what happened, Herald Loomis?

LOOMIS. They ain't moved or nothing. They just laying there.

BYNUM. You just laying there. (*Gestures and LOOMIS falls suddenly onto his back.*) What you waiting on, Herald Loomis?

LOOMIS. I'm laying there ... waiting.

BYNUM. What you waiting on, Herald Loomis?

LOOMIS. I'm waiting on the breath to get into my body.

BYNUM. The breath coming into you, Herald Loomis. What you gonna do now?

LOOMIS. (*Discovering.*) The wind's blowing the breath into my body. I can feel it. I'm starting to breath again.

BYNUM. What you gonna do, Herald Loomis?

LOOMIS. I'm gonna stand up. I got to stand up. I can't lay here no more. All the breath coming into my body and (*Rolls over onto his stomach.*) I got to stand up.

BYNUM. (*Throws his hands up overhead as LOOMIS scrambles up on all fours.*) Everybody's standing at the same time.

LOOMIS. (*Collapses, shakes.*) The ground's starting to shake. (*He grabs hold of the bench.*) There's a great shaking. (*He claws at the floor, arms open wide, trying to keep the ground together under him.*) The world's busting half in two. (*He flips over onto his back, looks up, sees the sky above him, tries to shield himself from it.*) The sky's splitting open. I got to stand up. (*Turns over, attempts to stand up, but his feet slide out from under him.*) My legs ... my legs won't stand up!

BYNUM. (*Points ahead of LOOMIS.*) Everybody's standing and walking toward the road. What you gonna do, Herald Loomis?

LOOMIS. (*Looks to BYNUM.*) My legs won't stand up.

BYNUM. They shaking hands and saying goodbye to each other and walking every whichway down the road.

LOOMIS. (*Tries to rise.*) I got to stand up! (*He cannot lift himself and collapses.*)

BYNUM. They walking around here now. Mens. Just like you and me. (*BYNUM throws his arms up overhead.*) Come right up out of the water.

LOOMIS. (*Becomes more and more frantic as he scrambles to stand and his feet slip out from under him each time.*) Got to stand up.

BYNUM. (*Reaches toward the "road" in front of LOOMIS.*) They walking, Herald Loomis. They walking around here now.

(*LOOMIS grabs one foot and pulls it up under him, retains his grip as he struggles to rise.*)

LOOMIS. I got to stand up. Get up on the road.

BYNUM. (*Reaches for LOOMIS, then throws his arms overhead.*) Comeon, Herald Loomis.

LOOMIS. (*Arcs up with one final supreme effort.*) My legs won't stand up!

(*LOOMIS's legs slide out from under him as he collapses onto his back, exhausted and with finality.*)

LOOMIS. My legs won't stand up!

(*BYNUM sags, defeated, against the kitchen table. He sits and looks up. LIGHTS: fade to black.*)

END OF ACT I

ACT II

Scene 1

SOUND: music up with LIGHTS: house lights and preset fade to black. SOUND: music fades out as LIGHTS: fade up in the kitchen. It is the next morning. BERTHA stands center stage looking at SETH. SETH sits in his chair, fuming. ZONIA sits on the porch railing, looks in the kitchen window at BERTHA. After a silence, BERTHA clears breakfast dishes from the table and moves to the sink.

SETH. I don't care what his problem is! He's leaving here!

BERTHA. (*Puts dishes down loudly in the sink.*) You can't put the man out and he got that little girl. Where they gonna go then?

SETH. (*Rises, paces around the kitchen table to the archway, upstage center.*) I don't care where he go. Let him go back where he was before he come here. I ain't asked him to come here. I knew when I first looked at him something wasn't right with him. Dragging that little girl around with him.

(BERTHA tries to shush him, and closes the window. ZONIA crosses to the porches steps dejectedly and sits.)

SETH. Looking like he be sleeping in the woods somewhere. I knew all along he wasn't right. (*Paces back to his chair.*)

BERTHA. A fellow get a little drunk he's liable to say or do anything. He ain't done no big harm.

SETH. (*Sits.*) I just don't have all that carrying on in my house. When he come down here I'm gonna tell him. He got to leave here. My daddy wouldn't stand for it and I ain't gonna stand for it either.

BERTHA. (*Crosses around his chair to confront SETH.*) Well if you put him out you have to put Bynum out too. Bynum right there with him.

SETH. If it wasn't for Bynum ain't no tell what would have happened. Bynum talked to that fellow just as nice and calmed him down. If he wasn't here ain't no telling what would have happened. Bynum ain't done nothing but talk to him and kept him calm. Man acting all crazy with that foolishness. Naw, he's leaving here.

BERTHA. What you gonna tell him. How you gonna tell him to leave?

SETH. I'm gonna tell him straight out. Keep it nice and simple. Mister, you got to leave here!

(*MOLLY enters the kitchen suddenly from the stairs.*)

MOLLY. Morning.

(*BERTHA startled, tries to recover her composure. She sets MOLLY's place upstage center at the kitchen table.*)

BERTHA. Did you sleep alright in that bed?

MOLLY. Tired as I was I could have slept anywhere. It's a real nice room though. This is a nice place. (*Sits at the table. BERTHA pours her coffee.*)

SETH. I'm sorry you had to put up with all that carrying on last night.

MOLLY. It don't bother me none. I done seen that kind of stuff before.

SETH. You won't have to see it around here no more. I don't put up with all that stuff. When that fellow come down here I'm gonna tell him.

(*BYNUM is heard singing upstairs. BERTHA sets his place at the table. He crosses down the stairs, and through the hall. He carries his basket of weeds.*)

BYNUM.
SOON MY WORK WILL ALL BE DONE
SOON MY WORK WILL ALL BE DONE
SOON MY WORK WILL ALL BE DONE
I'M GOING TO SEE THE KING.

(*BYNUM enters the kitchen carrying his basket. He places the basket in the upstage left corner of the kitchen on the floor.*)

BYNUM. Morning Seth. Morning, Sister Bertha. I see we got Molly Cunningham down here at breakfast.

(*BYNUM crosses to his chair at the table. SETH rises and moves to intercept him.*)

SETH. Bynum, I wanna thank you for talking to that fellow last night and calming him down. If you hadn't been here ain't no telling what might have happened. (*Looks pointedly at BERTHA.*)

BYNUM. (*Sits in his chair.*) Mr. Loomis alright, Seth. He just got a little excited.

SETH. (*Dissatisfied. Crosses to his chair and sits.*) Well, he can get excited somewhere else cause he leaving here.

(*MATTIE enters the kitchen from upstairs, carries her purse, hat and gloves.*)

BYNUM. Well, there's Mattie Campbell.

MATTIE. Good morning.

BERTHA. Sit on down there Mattie. I got some biscuits be ready in a minute. The coffee's hot. (*Sets MATTIE's place downstage right at the kitchen table.*)

MATTIE. Jeremy gone already?

BYNUM. Yeah, he leave out of here early. He got to be there when the sun come up.

(*MATTIE sits at her place at the table, puts her hat, purse and gloves down on the bench beside her.*)

BYNUM. Most working men got to be there when the sun come up. Everybody but Seth. Seth work at night. Mr. Olowski so busy in his shop he got fellows working at night.

(*LOOMIS enters suddenly from upstairs, moves through the hall and into the kitchen via the archway. SETH rises and blocks his path to the porch door. BERTHA stands between them, tending the stove.*)

SETH. Mr. Loomis, now ... I don't want no trouble. I keeps me a respectable house here. I don't have no carrying on like what went on last night. This has been a respectable house for a long time. I'm gonna have to ask you to leave.

LOOMIS. You got my two dollars. That two dollars say we stay till Saturday.

(*LOOMIS and SETH stare at each other.*)

SETH. Alright. Fair enough. You stay still Saturday. But come Saturday you got to leave here.

(*SETH crosses to his chair and sits. LOOMIS continues to glare at SETH, finally looks to BERTHA. She looks away. He goes to the porch door and opens it as she takes the biscuits out of the oven and puts them down on the center of the kitchen table. ZONIA rises and turns to LOOMIS.*)

LOOMIS. Zonia. You stay around this house. Don't you go nowhere.

(*ZONIA nods. LOOMIS caresses ZONIA on the forehead, abruptly steps back into the house and closes the porch door. He crosses rapidly through the kitchen and exits through the front door, slamming it closed behind him. ZONIA sits back down on the porch steps. BERTHA pours coffee for MATTIE and BYNUM.*)

SETH. (*Rises and paces above the table to the kitchen archway.*) I knew it when I first seen him. I knew something wasn't right with him. (*Continues to pace around downstage of the kitchen table rapidly.*)

BERTHA. Seth, leave the people alone to eat their breakfast. They don't want to hear that.

(*SETH arrives at the icebox and picks up his work gloves. He continues to pace.*)

BERTHA. (*Furious, and tries to contain it.*) Go on out there and make some pots and pans. That's the only time you satisfied is when you out there. Go on out there and make some pots and pans and leave them people alone.

SETH. (*Stops pacing and turns to her.*) I ain't bothering nobody. I'm just stating the facts. (*Points to BYNUM.*) I told you, Bynum.

(*SETH exits through the porch door, slams it behind him. BERTHA hesitates, embarrassed and upset, sets the coffee pot down heavily on the stove and exits quickly into the bedroom. She slams the door behind her. ZONIA more and more dejected, rises, crosses to the corner of the porch, and sits with her back to the railing. Long silence. MOLLY chooses a biscuit. She cuts it in half, butters it lavishly, then looks at BYNUM. She cuts it in quarters, then looks at BYNUM again. She puts down her knife and looks at BYNUM yet again.*)

MOLLY. (*To BYNUM.*) You one of them voo-doo people?

BYNUM. I got a power to bind folks if that what you talking about.

MOLLY. I thought so. The way you talked to that
man when he started all that spooky stuff. What you say
you had the power to do to people? You ain't the cause of
him acting like that is you?

BYNUM. I binds them together. Sometimes I help
them find each other.

MOLLY. How you do that?

BYNUM. With a song. My daddy taught me how to
do it.

MOLLY. That's what they say. Most folks be what
they daddy is. I wouldn't want to be like my daddy.
Nothing ever set right with him. He tried to make the
world over. Carry it around with him everywhere he go. I
don't want to be like that. I just take life as it come. I
don't be trying to make it over. (*Pause. MATTIE rises,
crosses to the icebox and looks out the kitchen window.
She waves to ZONIA.*) Your daddy used to do that too,
huh? Make people stay together.

BYNUM. My daddy used to heal people. He had the
Healing Song. I got the Binding Song.

(*MATTIE crosses over to the stove and watches MOLLY.*)

MOLLY. My mama used to believe in all that stuff. If
she got sick she would have gone and saw your daddy. As
long as he didn't make her drink nothing. She would drink
nothing nobody give her. She was always afraid somebody
was gonna poison her. How your daddy heal people?

BYNUM. With a song. He healed people by singing
over them. I seen him do it. He sung over this little white
girl when she was sick. They made a big to-do about it.
They carried the girl's bed out in the yard and had all her
kinfolk standing around. The little girl laying up there in

the bed. Doctors standing around can't do nothing to help her. And they had my daddy come up and sing his song. It didn't sound no different than any other song. It was just somebody singing. But the song was its own thing and it come out and took upon this little girl with its power and it healed her.

MOLLY. That's sure something else. I don't understand that kind of thing. I guess if the doctor couldn't make me well I'd try it. But otherwise I don't wanna be bothered with that kind of thing. It's too spooky.

BYNUM. (*Insulted, tries to hide it.*) Well let me get on out here and get to work.

(*BYNUM rises abruptly, crosses to the corner of the kitchen, and picks up his basket. He crosses to the porch door, gives a nod to MATTIE as he passes her.*)

MOLLY. (*As he goes.*) I ain't meant to offend you or nothing. What's your name ... Bynum? I ain't meant to say nothing to make you feel bad now.

(*BYNUM exits out the porch door.*)

MOLLY. (*To MATTIE.*) I hope he don't feel bad. He's a nice man. I don't wanna hurt nobody's feelings or nothing.

MATTIE. (*Crosses to the sink and washes her coffee cup.*) I got to get on up to Doc Goldblum's and finish this ironing.

MOLLY. Now that's something I don't never wanna do. Iron no clothes. Especially somebody else's. That's what I believe killed my mama. Always ironing and

working, doing somebody else's work. Not Molly
Cunningham.

(*MATTIE crosses to the kitchen table and picks up her
clean plate and silverware.*)

MATTIE. It's the only job I got. I got to make it
someway to fend for myself. (*Puts the plate and silverware
back on the side table upstage center, behind MOLLY.*)
MOLLY. I thought Jeremy was your man. Ain't he
working?
MATTIE. We just be keeping company until maybe
Jack come back. (*Crosses to the sink, washes her hands and
wets the dishrag.*)
MOLLY. I don't trust none of these men. Jack or
nobody else. These men liable to do anything. They wait
just until they get one woman tied and locked up with
them ... then they look around to see if they can get
another one. Molly don't pay them no mind. One's just as
good as the other if you ask me. I ain't never met one that
meant nobody no good.

(*MOLLY scoops butter up with her finger and licks it off,
as MATTIE crosses to the kitchen table, bends over
and brushes the crumbs off the table into her hand with
the dishrag.*)

MOLLY. You got any babies?
MATTIE. (*Rises.*) I had two for my man, Jack Carper.
But they both died. (*Crosses to the sink.*)
MOLLY. That be the best.

(*MATTIE turns to MOLLY in shock.*)

MOLLY. These men make all these babies then run off and leave you to take care of them. Talking about they wanna see what's on the other side of the hill. I make sure I don't get no babies. My mama taught me how to do that.

MATTIE. Don't make no mind. That be nice to be a mother.

MOLLY. Yeah? Well, you go on then. Molly Cunningham ain't gonna be tied down with no babies.

(*MATTIE turns quickly toward the sink, brushes the crumbs into the garbage can underneath, puts down the dishrag on the sink edge. She crosses rapidly to the bench, picks up her hat, gloves, and purse, and moves to the kitchen archway. MOLLY stares out, troubled.*)

MOLLY. Had me a man one time who I thought had some love in him.

(*MATTIE stops at the kitchen archway, her back to MOLLY.*)

MOLLY. Come home one day and he was packing his trunk. Told me the time come when even the best of friends must part. Say he was gonna send me a Special Delivery some old day. I watched him out the window when he carried that trunk out and down to the train station.

(*MOLLY's voice catches. She stops speaking, looks down at her lap, and smoothes her napkin. MATTIE turns to MOLLY and steps towards her. MOLLY looks up at MATTIE defiantly. MATTIE stops her cross.*)

MOLLY. Said if he was gonna send me a Special Delivery I wasn't gonna be there to get it. I done found out the harder you try to hold onto them, the easier it is for some gal to pull them away. Molly done learned that. (*Composed again.*) That's why I don't trust nobody but the good Lord above, and I don't love nobody but my mama.

MATTIE. I got to get on. (*Crosses to the hallway. Over her shoulder.*) Doc Goldblum gonna be waiting.

(*MATTIE crosses through the hallway and the front door, puts on her hat and gloves, and exits. Alone, MOLLY is again pained by her memory. SETH enters from his workshop through the porch door, wearing his work apron and gloves. His goggles are around his neck and he carries an empty pail. He crosses to the sink.*)

SETH. Everybody gone but you, huh? (*Puts the bucket down in the sink, turns the water on to fill it.*)

MOLLY. (*Quickly recovers.*) That little shack out there by the outhouse ... that's where you make them pots and pans and stuff?

SETH. (*Flattered and proud.*) Yep. That's my workshed. I go out there ... take these hands and make something out of nothing. Take that metal and bend and twist it whatever way I want. My daddy taught me that. He used to make pots and pans. That's how I learned it.

MOLLY. I never knew nobody make no pots and pans. My uncle used to shoe horses.

(*JEREMY enters suddenly through the porch door, crosses directly to the kitchen archway heading for the stairs ...*)

SETH. (*Surprised to see him.*) I thought you was working? Ain't you working today?

JEREMY. (*Turns to SETH. Vehemently.*) Naw, they fired me.

(*SETH turns the water off.*)

JEREMY. White fellow come by told me to give him fifty cents if I wanted to keep working. Going around to all the colored making them give him fifty cents to keep hold to their jobs. Them other fellows, they was giving it to him. I kept hold to mine and they fired me. (*Turns to go, stops when SETH calls to him.*)

SETH. Boy, what kind of sense that make. What kind of sense it make to get fired from a job where you making eight dollars a week and all it cost you is fifty cents. That's seven dollars and fifty cents profit! This way you ain't got nothing.

JEREMY. (*Crosses downstage left of the table, level with SETH.*) It didn't make no sense to me. I don't make but eight dollars. Why I got to give him fifty cents of it? He go around to all the colored and he got ten dollars extra. That's more than I make for a whole week.

SETH. (*Steps in to the table, toward JEREMY.*) I see you gonna learn the hard way. You just looking at the facts of it. See, right now, without the job you ain't got nothing. What you gonna do when you can't keep a roof over your head? Right now, come Saturday, unless you come up with another two dollars, you gonna be out there in the streets. Down up under one of them bridges trying to put dome food in your belly and wishing you had given that fellow that fifty cents.

JEREMY. (*Crosses away downstage center.*) Don't make me no difference. There's a big road out there.

(*MOLLY laughs out loud, tries to stifle it. SETH crosses to the sink and picks up the pail of water.*)

JEREMY. I can get my guitar and always find me another place to stay. I ain't planning on staying in one place too long noway.
SETH. We gonna see if you feel like that come Saturday!

(*SETH crosses through the porch door, starts down the steps, stops, turns to ZONIA, gestures for her to come along. He exits stage right. She happily follows him off to exit upstage right. JEREMY turns to see MOLLY sipping her coffee and takes off his cap.*)

JEREMY. (*Flirting.*) Molly Cunningham.

(*JEREMY crosses to the table, pulls out the stage left chair, turns it around, and sits, straddling it. He hangs his hat on the chair back.*)

JEREMY. How you doin' today, sugar?
MOLLY. (*Stacking her plate, knife and napkin carefully. Matter-of-fact.*) You can go on back down there tomorrow and go back to work if you want. They won't even know who you is. Won't even know it's you. I had me a fellow did that one time. They just went ahead and signed him up like they never seen him before.
JEREMY. I'm tired of working anyway. I'm glad they fired me. You sure look pretty today.

MOLLY. Don't come telling me all that pretty stuff. Beauty wanna come in and sit down at your table asking to be fed. I ain't hardly got enough for me.

JEREMY. (*Disbelieving.*) You know you pretty. Ain't no sense in you saying nothing about that. Why don't you come and go away with me?

MOLLY. (*Angrily.*) You tied up with that Mattie Campbell. Now you talking about running away with me.

JEREMY. I was just keeping her company cause she lonely. You ain't the lonely kind. You the kind that know what she want and how to get it. I need a woman like you to travel around and look at some places. Don't you want to travel around and look at some places with Jeremy? With a woman like you beside him, a man can make it nice in the world.

MOLLY. (*Dismissing him.*) Molly can make it nice by herself too. Molly don't need nobody leave her cold in hand. The world rough enough as it is.

JEREMY. We can make it better together. I got my guitar and I can play. Won me another dollar last night playing the guitar.

(*MOLLY turns away, sips coffee.*)

JEREMY. We can go around and I can play at the dances and we can just enjoy life. You can make it by yourself alright, I agrees with that. A woman like you can make it anywhere she go. But you can make it better if you got a man to protect you.

MOLLY. (*With a sudden interest.*) What places you wanna go around and look at?

JEREMY. All of them.

(*MOLLY laughs, JEREMY jumps up.*)

JEREMY. I don't want to miss nothing. I wanna go everywhere and do everything there is to be got out of life. With a woman like you it's like having water and berries. A man got everything he need.

MOLLY. (*Sizes him up.*) You got to be doing more than playing that guitar. A dollar a day ain't hardly what Molly got in mind.

JEREMY. I gambles real good. I got a hand for it.

MOLLY. (*Drives a hard bargain.*) Molly don't work. And Molly ain't up for sale.

JEREMY. (*Pulls a few bills out of his overall pockets.*) Sure baby, you ain't got to work with Jeremy.

MOLLY. There's one more thing.

JEREMY. What's that sugar?

MOLLY. (*Faces out.*) Molly ain't going South.

(*MOLLY rises slowly, crosses to JEREMY, picks up his hat from the chair back and holds it out to him. As he takes it, SOUND: music starts. MOLLY crosses past JEREMY and exits up the stairs. He lets out a whoop of joy, slaps the cap against his thigh, and follows her up the stairs to exit as the LIGHTS: fade to black with SOUND: music swells.*)

ACT II

Scene

SOUND: music fades out as LIGHTS: fade up in the parlor and, dimly, in the kitchen, It is Monday evening. SETH on the love seat and BYNUM on the stage right chair sit playing a game of dominoes at the parlor table. BYNUM sings to himself.

BYNUM. (*Singing.*)
THEY TELL ME JOE TURNER'S COME AND GONE
OHHH LORDY
THEY TELL ME JOE TURNER'S COME AND GONE
OHHH LORDY
GOT MY MAN AND GONE

COME WITH FORTY LINKS OF CHA'N
OHHH LORDY
COME WITH FORTY LINKS OF CHAIN
OHHH LORDY
GOT MY MAN AND GONE

SETH. (*Impatiently.*) Comeon and play if you gonna play.
BYNUM. I'm gonna play. Soon as I figure out what to do.
SETH. You can't figure out if you wanna play or you wanna sing.
BYNUM. Well sir, I'm gonna do a little bit of both. (*Plays. Delighted with himself.*) There. What you gonna do now? (*Singing.*)
THEY TELL ME JOE TURNER'S COME AND GONE
OHHH LORDY
THEY TELL ME JOE TURNER'S COME AND GONE
OHHH LORDY
SETH. Why don't you hush up that noise.

BYNUM. That's a song the women sing down around Memphis. The women down there made up that song. I picked it up down there about fifteen years ago.

(*LOOMIS enters through the front door.*)

BYNUM. Evening, Mr. Loomis.

(*LOOMIS closes the door and crosses to the stairs.*)

SETH. Today's Monday, Mr. Loomis. Come Saturday your time is up. We done ate already. My wife roasted up some yams. She got your plate sitting in there on the table.

(*LOOMIS hesitates, crosses through the hallway and into the kitchen.*)

SETH. (*To BYNUM.*) Whose play is it?
BYNUM. Ain't you keeping up with the game? I thought you was a domino player. I just played so it got to be your turn.

(*LOOMIS, still standing, uncovers the plate of yams set at the stage left end of the table. He sits down and begins to eat with his hands, voraciously. SETH plays decisively.*)

SETH. Twenty! Give me twenty! You didn't know I had that ace five. You was trying to play around that. You didn't know I had that lying there for you.
BYNUM. You ain't done nothing. I let you have that to get mine.

SETH. Comeon and play. You ain't doing nothing but talking. I got a hundred and forty points to your eight. You ain't doin nothing but talking. Comeon and play.

BYNUM. (*Singing.*)
THEY TELL ME JOE TURNER'S COME AND GONE
OHHH LORDY

(*LOOMIS stops eating, frozen.*)

BYNUM.
THEY TELL ME JOE TURNER'S COME AND GONE
OHH LORDY
GOT MY MAN AND GONE

(*LOOMIS puts his glass of lemonade down, rises and moves quickly to the sliding door.*)

BYNUM.
HE COMES WITH FORTY LINKS OF CHAIN
OHHH LORDY

(*LOOMIS opens sliding door forcefully, crosses in to stand over BYNUM.*)

LOOMIS. I don't like you singing that song, mister!

SETH. Now I ain't gonna have no more disturbance around here, Herald Loomis. You start any more disturbances and you leaving here. Saturday or no Saturday.

BYNUM. The man ain't causing no disturbance, Seth. He just say he don't like the song.

SETH. Well, we all friendly folk. All neighborly like. Don't have no squabbling around here. Don't have no disturbance. You gonna have to take that someplace else.

BYNUM. He just say he don't like the song. I done sung a whole lot of songs people don't like. I respect everybody. He here in the house too. If he don't like the song, I'll sing something else.

(*LOOMIS turns away and crosses slowly back to his chair at the kitchen table.*)

BYNUM. I know a lot of songs. You got, "I Belong to the Band", "Don't you Leave Me Here". You got, "Praying on the Old Campground", "Keep Your Lamp Trimmed and Burning" ... I know lots of songs.

(*LOOMIS sits.*)

BYNUM. (*Singing. Clapping and stomping.*)
BOYS I'LL BE SO GLAD WHEN PAYDAY COME
CAPTAIN, CAPTAIN, WHEN PAYDAY COME
GONNA CATCH THAT ILLINOIS CENTRAL
GOING TO KANKAKEE
SETH. (*Interrupting.*) Why don't you hush up that hollering and comeon and play dominoes.
BYNUM. (*Turns to LOOMIS.*) You ever been to Johnstown, Herald Loomis? You look like a fellow I seen around there.
LOOMIS. I don't know no place with that name.
BYNUM. That's around where I seen my shiny man. See, you looking for this woman. I'm looking for a shiny man. Seem like everybody looking for something.
SETH. I'm looking for you to come on and play these dominoes. That's what I'm looking for.
BYNUM. You a farming man, Herald Loomis? You look like you done some farming.

LOOMIS. Same as everybody. I done farmed some, yeah.

BYNUM. I used to work at farming ... picking cotton. I reckon everybody done picked some cotton.

SETH. I ain't! I ain't never picked no cotton. I was born up here in the North. My daddy was a freedman. I ain't never even seen no cotton!

BYNUM. Mr. Loomis done picked some cotton. Ain't you, Herald Loomis. You done picked a bunch of cotton.

LOOMIS. How you know so much about me? How you know what I done? How much cotton I picked?

BYNUM. I can tell from looking at you. My daddy taught me how to do that. Say when you look at a fellow, if you taught youself to look for it, you can see his song written on him. Tell you what kind of man he is in the world. Now I can look at you, Mr. Loomis, and see you a man who done forgot his song. Forgot how to sing it. A fellow forget that and he forget who he is. Forget how he's supposed to mark down life. Now I used to travel all up and down this road and that ... looking here and there. Searching. Just like you, Mr. Loomis ... I didn't know what I was searching for. The only thing I knew was something was keeping me dissatisfied. Something wasn't making my heart smooth and easy. Then one day my daddy gave me a song. That song had a weight to it that was hard to handle. That song was hard to carry.

(*LOOMIS stops eating.*)

BYNUM. I fought against it. Didn't want to accept that song. I tried to find my daddy to give him back the song. But I found out it wasn't his song. It was my song. It had come from way deep inside me. I looked way back in my memory and gathered up pieces and snatches of things to make that song. I was making it up out of myself. And that song helped me on the road. (*Rises and crosses slowly to above the kitchen table.*) Made it smooth to where my footsteps didn't bite back at me. All the time that song getting bigger and bigger. That song growing with each step of the road. It got so I used all of myself up in the making of that song. Then I was the song in search of itself. That song rattling in my throat and I'm looking for it. (*Turns, pulls out a chair, and sits, facing LOOMIS.*) See, Mr. Loomis, when a man forgets his song he goes off in search of it ... till he finds out he's got it with him all the time. That's why I can tell you one of Joe Turner's niggers. Cause you forgot how to sing your song.

LOOMIS. (*Lunges suddenly for BYNUM, who does not flinch, yet LOOMIS does not reach him.*) You lie! How you see that? I got a mark on me? Joe Turner done marked me to where you can see it? You telling me I'm a marked man. What kind of mark you got on you?

(*LOOMIS is stunned by BYNUM's revelation. BYNUM doesn't respond. BYNUM begins singing.*)

BYNUM.
THEY TELL ME JOE TURNER'S COME AND GONE
OHHH LORDY

(*Rises slowly.*)

THEY TELL ME JOE TURNER'S COME AND GONE
OHHH LORDY

(*Crosses slowly to his chair in the parlor, turns it out to face LOOMIS, and sits.*)

GOT MY MAN AND GONE

LOOMIS. Had a whole mess of men he catched. Just go out hunting regular like you go out hunting possum. He catch you and go home to his wife and family. Ain't thought about you going home to yours. Joe Turner catched me when my little girl was just born. Wasn't nothing but a little baby sucking on her mama's titty when he catched me. Joe Turner catched me in nineteen hundred and one. Kept me seven years until nineteen hundred and eight, kept everybody seven years. He'd go out hunting and bring back forty men a a time. And keep them seven years. I was walking down this road in this little town outside of Memphis. Comeup on these fellows gambling. I was a deacon in the Abundant Life Church. I stopped to preach to these fellows to see if I could turn some of them from their sinning when Joe Turner – brother of the Governor of the Great Sovereign State of Tennessee – swooped down and grabbed everybody there. Kept us all seven years.

(*MATTIE enters from upstairs, in her nightgown. She slowly crosses downstairs to the landing.*)

LOOMIS. My wife Martha gone from me after Joe Turner catched me. Got out from under Joe Turner on his birthday. Me and forty other men put in our seven years and he let us go on his birthday. I made it back to Henry Thompson's place where me and Martha was sharecropping and Martha's gone. She taken my little girl and left her with her mama and took off North. We been looking for her ever since.

(*MATTIE slows crosses through the hall to the kitchen archway, watches LOOMIS.*)

LOOMIS. That's been going on four years now we been looking. That's the only thing I know how to do I just wanna see her face so I can get me a starting place in the world. The world got to start somewhere. That's what I been looking for. I been wandering a long time in somebody else's world. When I find my wife that be the making of my own.

BYNUM. Joe Turner tell why he caught you? You ever asked him that?

LOOMIS. I ain't never seen Joe Turner. Seen him to where I could touch him. I asked one of them fellows one time why he catch niggers. Asked him what I got he want? Why don't he keep on to himself? Why he got to catch me going down the road by my lonesome. He told me I was worthless. Worthless is something you throw away. Something you don't bother with. I ain't seen him throw me away. Wouldn't even let me stay away when I was by my lonesome. I ain't tried to catch him when he going down the road. So I must got something he want. What I got?

SETH. (*Simply.*) He just want you to do his work for him. That's all.

LOOMIS. I can look at him and see where he big and strong enough to do his own work. So it can't be that. He must want something he ain't got.

BYNUM. That ain't hard to figure out. What he wanted was your song. He wanted to have that song to be his. He thought by catching you he could learn that song. Every nigger he catch he's looking for the one he can learn that song from. Now he's got you bound up to where you can't sing your own song. Couldn't sing it them seven years cause you was afraid he would snatch it from under you. But you still got it. You just forgot how to sing it.

(*LOOMIS rises suddenly. MATTIE crosses quickly into the pantry, still watching LOOMIS.*)

LOOMIS. (*To BYNUM.*) I know who you are. You one of them bones people.

(*SOUND: the music starts as LOOMIS turns to go and sees MATTIE suddenly turn away, pretending to look for something in the pantry. LOOMIS hesitates, quickly crosses through the hallway, then exits up the stairs. MATTIE follows LOOMIS to the hallway and watches him exit. BYNUM pulls off his beads in a clenched fist, breaking them, as the LIGHTS: fade to black and SOUND: music swells.*)

ACT II

Scene 3

SOUND: music fades out as LIGHTS: fade up in the kitchen. It is the following morning. MATTIE sits on the bench, and BYNUM sits in his chair at the table. BERTHA fixes LOOMIS a bowl of grits at the stove.

BYNUM. Good luck don't know no special time to come. You sleep with that up under your pillow and good luck can't help but come to you. Sometime it come and go and you don't even know it's been there.

(*MATTIE turns away from him, facing out.*)

BERTHA. (*Intervenes.*) Bynum, why don't you leave that gal alone. She don't wanna be hearing all that. Why don't you go on and get out the way and leave her alone.

BYNUM. (*Rising.*) Alright ... alright. (*Unable to resist. Leans over to MATTIE.*) But you mark what I'm saying. It'll draw it to you just like a magnet.

(*LOOMIS enters the kitchen from upstairs, intercepts BYNUM as he turns to go. They exchange a long look. BYNUM finally crosses to the corner of the kitchen picks up his basket, crosses half-way up the stairs, stops to listen.*)

BERTHA. (*Sets LOOMIS breakfast at the stage left place on the kitchen table.*) I got some grits here, Mr. Loomis. (*Continues her cross around the table, sits next to MATTIE on the bench. BYNUM exits upstairs.*) If I was you, Mattie, I wouldn't go getting all tied up with Bynum in that stuff. That kind of stuff, even if it do work for awhile, it don't last. That just get people more mixed up than they is already. And I wouldn't waste my time fretting over Jeremy either. I seen it coming. I seen it when she first come here. She that kind of woman run off with the first man got a dollar to spend on her. Jeremy just young. He don't know what he getting into. That gal don't mean him no good. She's just using him to keep from being by herself. That's the worse kind of a man you can have.

(LOOMIS sits and begins to eat his breakfast.)

BERTHA. You ought to be glad to wash him out of your hair. I done seen all kind of men. I done seen them come and go through here. Jeremy ain't had enough to him for you. You need a man who's got some understanding and who willing to work with that understand to come to the best he can. You got your time coming. You just tries too hard and can't understand why it don't work for you. Trying to figure it out don't do nothing but give you a troubled mind. Don't no man want a woman with a troubled mind.

You get all that trouble off your mind and just when it look like you ain't never gonna find what you want ... you look up and it's standing right there. That's how I met my Seth. You gonna look up one day and find everything you want standing right in front of you. Been twenty-seven years now since that happened to me. But life ain't no happy-go-lucky time where everything be just like you want it. You got your time coming.

(BERTHA takes MATTIE's hand in hers as SETH enters through the porch door with his lunch pail and work gloves.)

BERTHA. You watch what Bertha's saying.
SETH. *(Puts his lunch pail and work gloves down on the icebox.)* Ho!
BERTHA. *(With a wink to MATTIE.)* What you doing come in here so late?

SETH. (*Hangs his hat on the hook over the icebox.*) I was standing down there on Logan Street talking with the fellows. Henry Allen tried to sell me that old piece of horse he got. (*Turns to see LOOMIS.*) Today's Tuesday, Mr. Loomis.

BERTHA. (*Rises, crosses to SETH, takes his hand, and pulls him toward the bedroom.*) Seth, comeon in here and leave the man alone to eat his breakfast.

SETH. I ain't bothering nobody. I'm just reminding him what day it is.

(*BERTHA and SETH exit into their bedroom. BERTHA closes the door. After a moment, MATTIE stirs.*)

LOOMIS. That dress got a color to it.

MATTIE. (*Still seated, turns to him.*) Did you really see them things like you said? Them people come up out the ocean?

LOOMIS. It happened just like that, yeah.

MATTIE. I hope you find your wife. It be good for your little girl for you to find her.

LOOMIS. Got to find her for myself. Find my starting place in the world. Find me a world I can fit in.

MATTIE. I ain't never found no place for me to fit. Seems like all I do is start over. It ain't nothing to find no starting place in the world. You just start from where you find yourself.

LOOMIS. Got to find my wife. That be my starting place.

MATTIE. What if you don't find her? What you gonna do then if you don't find her?

LOOMIS. She out there somewhere. Ain't no such thing as not finding her.

MATTIE. How she get lost from you? Jack just walked away from me.

LOOMIS. Joe Turner split us up. Joe Turner turned the world upside down. He bound me on to him for seven years.

MATTIE. I hope you find her. It be good for you to find her. (*Rises, turns and reaches for her plate.*)

LOOMIS. I been watching you. I been watching you watch me.

MATTIE. (*Picks up her plate, silverware and cup.*) I was just trying to figure out if you seen them things like you said. (*Crosses to the sink, puts down her breakfast dishes in it.*)

LOOMIS. Come here and let me touch you. I been watching you. You a full woman. A man needs a full woman. Comeon and be with me.

MATTIE. (*Turns to him.*) I ain't got enough for you. You'd use me up too fast.

LOOMIS. (*Rises slowly.*) Herald Loomis got a mind seem like you part of it since I first seen you. It's been a long time since I seen a full woman. I can smell you from here. (*Crosses slowly toward MATTIE.*) I know you got Herald Loomis on your mind, can't keep him apart from it. Comeon and be with Herald Loomis.

(*LOOMIS steps in to MATTIE, reaches out slowly, awkwardly, gently, tenderly. Inside he howls like a lost wolf pup whose hunger is deep. His hand starts to shake. He recoils, grabbing his shaking hand with his other hand.*)

LOOMIS. I done forgot how to touch.

(*LOOMIS turns abruptly, exits rapidly through the front door. ZONIA enters the backyard, singing "Just a pullin the skiff ..." She follows the path to the corner of the porch. MATTIE watches LOOMIS go, hesitates, then crosses to the porch door. ZONIA stops singing, turns to her and waves as MATTIE opens the door. MATTIE stops, closes the door, and exits quickly through the hallway and upstairs. LIGHTS: crossfade to the path and the cellar door as SOUND: birds chirp intermittently outside.*)

ACT II

Scene 4

ZONIA starts to sing again, crosses quickly around the porch to the path to see if anyone is there. Find no one, she slows down, stops singing, and crosses slowly and sadly to the cellar door. She sits. REUBEN enters, running from the backyard, crosses to ZONIA.

REUBEN. (*Out of breath.*) Something spookly going on around here. Last night Mr. Bynum was out in the yard singing and talking to the wind ... and the wind it just be talking back to him. Did you hear it?

ZONIA. I heard it. I was scared to get up and look. I thought it was a storm.

REUBEN. That wasn't no storm. That was Mr. Bynum. First he say something ... and the wind say back to him. And this morning ... I seen Miss Mabel!

ZONIA. Who Miss Mabel?

REUBEN. Mr. Seth's mother. He got her picture hanging up in the house. She been dead.

ZONIA. How you seen her if she been dead?

REUBEN. Zonia ... if I tell you something you promise you won't tell anybody? (*Crosses his heart.*)

ZONIA. (*Crosses her heart.*) I promise.

REUBEN. It was early this morning ... I went out to the coop to feed the pigeons. I was down on the ground like this to open up the door to the coop ... (*Crouches low to the ground, reaches out.*) when all of a sudden I seen these feets in front of me. I looked up ... (*Looks up.*) and there was Miss Mabel standing there. (*Rises.*)

ZONIA. Reuben, you better stop telling that! You ain't seen nobody!

REUBEN. Naw, it's the truth I swear! I seen her just like I see you. Look ... you can see where she hit me with her cane. (*Sits next to ZONIA on the cellar door, holds out his arm to show her his bruises.*)

ZONIA. (*Grabs his arm to look at the bruises.*) Hit you? What she hit you for? (*Releases his arm.*)

REUBEN. She say, "Didn't you promise Eugene something?" Then she hit me with her cane. She say, "Let them pigeons go." Then she hit me again. That's what made them marks.

ZONIA. (*Inches away from him.*) Jeez man ... get away from me. You done see a haunt!

REUBEN. (*Looks around toward the path.*) Shhh. You promised, Zonia!

ZONIA. You sure it wasn't Miss Bertha come over there and hit you with her hoe?

REUBEN. It wasn't no Miss Bertha. I told you it was Miss Mabel. She was standing right there by the coop. She had this light coming out of her and then she just melted away. (*Falls back "melted."*)

ZONIA. What she had on?

REUBEN. (*Sits up.*) A white dress. Ain't even had no shoes or nothing. Just had on that white dress and them big hands ... and that cane she hit me with.

ZONIA. How you reckon she knew about the pigeons?

REUBEN. I don't know. I sure ain't asked her none. She say Eugene was waiting on them pigeons. Say he couldn't go home till I let them go. I couldn't get the door to the coop open fast enough.

ZONIA. You reckon Eugene the one who sent old Miss Mabel?

REUBEN. Why he send her. Why he don't come himself?

ZONIA. Figured if he send her maybe that'll make you listen cause she old.

REUBEN. (*Suddenly excited.*) If Miss Mabel can come back ... then maybe Eugene can come back too. We can go down to the hideout just like we used to! He could come back everyday! It be just like he ain't dead.

ZONIA. Maybe that ain't right for him to come back. Feel kinda funny to be playing games with a haunt.

REUBEN. Yeah ... what if everybody came back. What if Miss Mabel came back just like she ain't dead. Where you and your daddy gonna sleep then?

ZONIA. Maybe they go back at night and don't need no place to sleep.

REUBEN. It still don't seem right. I'm sure gonna miss Eugene. He's the bestest friend anybody ever had.

ZONIA. My daddy say if you miss somebody too much it can kill you. Say he missed me till it liked to killed him.

REUBEN. What if your mama's already dead and all the time you looking for her?

ZONIA. Naw, she ain't dead. My daddy say he can smell her.

REUBEN. You can't smell nobody that ain't here. (*Teasing.*) Maybe he smelling old Miss Bertha. Maybe Bertha your mama?

ZONIA. Naw, she ain't. My mama got long pretty hair and she five feet from the ground!

REUBEN. Your daddy say when you leaving?

(*ZONIA doesn't respond, looks away.*)

REUBEN. Maybe you gonna stay in Mr. Seth's house and don't go looking for your mama no more.

ZONIA. He say we got to leave on Saturday.

REUBEN. (*Surprised and disappointed.*) Dag! You just only been here for a little while. Don't seem like nothing ever stay the same.

ZONIA. He say he got to find her. Find him a place in the world.

REUBEN. He could find him a place in Mr. Seth's house.

ZONIA. (*Sorrowfully.*) It don't look like we never gonna find her.

REUBEN. Maybe he find her by Saturday then you don't have to go.

ZONIA. I don't know.

REUBEN. (*Teasing.*) You look like a spider!

ZONIA. (*Defensive.*) I ain't no spider!

REUBEN. Got them long skinny arms and legs. You look like one of them Black Widows.

ZONIA. I ain't no Black Widow nothing! My name is Zonia!

REUBEN. That's what I'm gonna call you ... Spider.

ZONIA. You can call me that, but I don't have to answer.

REUBEN. You know what? I think maybe I be your husband when I grow up.

ZONIA. How you know?

REUBEN. I ask my grandpap how you know and he say when the moon falls into a girl's eyes that how you know.

ZONIA. (*Leans over to him.*) Did it fall into my eyes?

REUBEN. (*Looks into her eyes, but doesn't see anything.*) Not that I can tell. Maybe I ain't old enough. Maybe you ain't old enough.

ZONIA. So there! I don't know why you telling me that lie!

REUBEN. That don't mean nothing cause I can't see it. I know it's there. Just the way you look at me sometimes look like the moon might have been in your eyes.

ZONIA. That don't mean nothing if you can't see it. You supposed to see it.

REUBEN. Shucks, I see it good enough for me. You ever let anybody kiss you?

ZONIA. Just my daddy. He kiss me on the cheek.

REUBEN. It's better on the lips. Can I kiss you on the lips?

ZONIA. I don't know. You ever kiss anybody before?

REUBEN. I had a cousin let me kiss her on the lips one time. Can I kiss you?

ZONIA. Okay.

(*REUBEN kisses her and lays his head against her chest. ZONIA looks down at him.*)

    ZONIA. What you doing?
    REUBEN. (*Sits up.*) Listening. Your heart singing!
    ZONIA. It is not.
    REUBEN. Just beating like a drum. Let's kiss again. (*They kiss again, this time ZONIA helps. REUBEN sits up.*) Now you mine, Spider. You my girl, okay?
    ZONIA. Okay.
    REUBEN. When I get grown, I come looking for you.
    ZONIA. Okay.

(*REUBEN lays his head down on her chest. SOUND: music starts as LIGHTS: fade to black.*)

ACT II

Scene 5

SOUND: music fades out as LIGHTS: fade up in the kitchen. It is Saturday morning. BYNUM sits in his chair at the table. BERTHA fixes ZONIA's breakfast at the stove and sets it on the kitchen table. She crosses to the icebox and pours a glass of milk. LOOMIS and ZONIA stand at the stage left end of the kitchen table. ZONIA is wearing a white dress, and carries her bundle. LOOMIS holds her hand. It is virtually the same position they were in when they arrived in the first scene.

BYNUM. With all this rain we been having he might have ran into some washed out roads. If that wagon got stuck in the mud he's liable to be still upriver somewhere. If he's upriver then he ain't coming until tomorrow.

LOOMIS. Today's Saturday. He say he be here on Saturday.

BERTHA. (*Crosses to the table and puts down the glass of milk.*) Zonia, you gonna eat your breakfast this morning?

ZONIA. Yes ma'am.

(*BERTHA watches ZONIA. She steps forward to cross to the table. LOOMIS does not release her hand. ZONIA steps back.*)

BERTHA. I don't see how you expect to get any bigger if you don't eat. I ain't never seen a child that didn't eat. You about as skinny as a pole bean.

(*Pause. LOOMIS releases ZONIA's hand. She crosses to the table, sits on the bench, and begins to eat her breakfast.*)

BERTHA. Mr. Loomis, there's a place down on Wylie. Zeke Mayweather got a house down there. You ought to see if he got any rooms. (*LOOMIS doesn't respond. BERTHA turns back to the stove. Over her shoulder.*) Well, you're welcome to some breakfast before you move on.

(*MATTIE enters from upstairs, crosses to the kitchen archway.*)

MATTIE. Good morning.

BERTHA. Morning, Mattie. Sit on down there and get you some breakfast.

(*MATTIE crosses above the table to the stage right end of the kitchen.*)

BYNUM. Well, Mattie Campbell, you been sleeping with that up under your pillow like I told you?

BERTHA. (*Crosses to BYNUM.*) Bynum, I done told you to leave that gal alone with all that stuff. You around here meddling in other people's lives. She don't want to hear all that. You ain't doing nothing but confusing her with that stuff.

MATTIE. (*To LOOMIS.*) You all fixing to move on?

LOOMIS. Today's Saturday. I'm paid up till Saturday.

(*BERTHA crosses back to the stove, takes a pan of biscuits out of the oven.*)

MATTIE. Where you going to?

LOOMIS. Gonna find my wife.

MATTIE. You going off to another city?

(*BERTHA puts the biscuits down on the stove top.*)

LOOMIS. We gonna see where the road take us. Ain't no telling where we wind up.

MATTIE. Eleven years is a long time. Your wife ... she might have taken up with someone else. People do that when they get lost from each other.

LOOMIS. Zonia. (*Holds out his hand to her.*) Comeon, we gonna find you mama.

(*ZONIA slowly picks up her bundle and rises. LOOMIS turns and crosses to the parlor archway. ZONIA crosses to the end of the bench as BERTHA moves down to her. They embrace. BERTHA breaks the embrace and backs away to the kitchen archway.*)

MATTIE. Zonia. (ZONIA *turns to her. MATTIE holds up a white bow.*) Mattie got a ribbon here match your dress. Want Mattie to fix your hair with her ribbon? (*ZONIA nods. MATTIE crosses to above ZONIA, turns her to face out. MATTIE ties the bow in her hair.*) There ... (*MATTIE turns ZONIA to face her. Embraces her.*) it got a color just like your dress.

(*MATTIE looks to LOOMIS as BERTHA turns away and dries her eyes on her handkerchief.*)

MATTIE. I hope you find her. I hope you be happy.

(*MATTIE releases ZONIA from the embrace and turns away. ZONIA crosses past LOOMIS to the front door, and leans forlornly against it.*)

LOOMIS. A man looking for a woman be lucky to find you.

(*MATTIE turns to him.*)

LOOMIS. You a good woman, Mattie. Keep a good heart.

(*LOOMIS turns, crosses to the front door, opens it, sends ZONIA through, and closes the door behind him. They exit stage left, hand in hand. MATTIE crosses slowly to the bench, and collapses to sit.*)

BYNUM. I been watching that man for two weeks ... and that's the closest I come to seeing him act civilized. I don't know what's between you all, Mattie ... but the only thing that man needs is somebody to make him laugh. That's all you need in the world is love and laughter. That's all anybody needs. To have love in one hand and laughter in the other.

(*BERTHA waves her handkerchief in the air, flicks it at BYNUM. He ducks and laughs. She continues to move about the kitchen as though blessing it and chasing away the huge sadness that seems to envelope it. It is a dance and demonstration of her own magic, her own remedy that is centuries old and to which she is connected by the muscles of her heart and the blood's memory.*)

BYNUM. You hear me, Mattie? I'm talking about laughing. The kind of laugh that comes from way deep inside. To just stand and laugh and let life flow right through you. Just laugh to let yourself know you're alive.

(*BERTHA laughs, jumps up and down and waves her handkerchief in the air. It is a near hysterical laughter that is a celebration of life, both its pain and its blessing. MATTIE and BYNUM join in the laughter. BERTHA reaches her arms out to MATTIE. MATTIE rises, crosses to BERTHA. They embrace. SETH enters through the porch door, drops his work gloves, lunch pail and hat on the icebox and continues to the table. He takes it all in and begins to laugh with them.)*

SETH. Well, I see you all having fun.

(BERTHA, MATTIE, and BYNUM laugh harder.)

SETH. That Loomis fellow standing up there on the corner watching the house.

(ALL stop laughing except SETH. BERTHA and MATTIE break embrace. BERTHA dries her eyes.)

SETH. He standing right up there on Manilla Street.
BERTHA. Don't you get started on him. The man done left out of here and that's the last I wanna hear of it. You about to drive me crazy with that man. *(BERTHA turns to the sink, washes her face and dries it with her handkerchief.)*
SETH. I just say he standing up there on the corner. Acting sneaky like he always do. He can stand up there all he want. As long as he don't come back in here.

(There is a knock on the front door. SETH goes to answer it. MATTIE moves below the stove, expectantly. MARTHA LOOMIS [PENTECOST] enters. She is a young woman about twenty-eight. She is dressed as befitting a member of an Evangelist church and carries a Bible.)

SETH. Look here, Bertha, It's Martha Pentecost. Comeon in Martha.

(*MARTHA crosses through the parlor into the kitchen.*)

SETH. Who that with you?

(*RUTHERFORD SELIG follows into the hallway.*)

SETH. Oh ... that's Selig. Comeon in Selig.
BERTHA. (*Joyful.*) Martha, comeon in.

(*MARTHA goes to BERTHA. They embrace as SETH closes the door and crosses into the kitchen, and SELIG moves into the parlor archway.*)

BERTHA. It's sure good to see you.
BYNUM. Rutherford Selig you a sure enough First Class People Finder!
SELIG. She was right out there in Rankin. You take that first right hand road ... right there at that church on Wooster Street. I started to go right past and something told me to stop at the church and see if they needed any dustpans.
SETH. Don't she look good, Bertha?
BERTHA. (*Breaks embrace, steps back to look at MARTHA.*) Look all nice and healthy.
MARTHA. (*Turns to BYNUM.*) Mr. Bynum ... Selig told me my little girl was here.

(*SELIG crosses to the love seat in the parlor, drops his hat on the table, and sits.*)

SETH. There's some fellow around here say he is your husband. Say his name is Loomis. Say you his wife.

MARTHA. Is my little girl with him?

SETH. Yeah he got a little girl with him. I wasn't gonna tell him where you was. Not the way this fellow look. So he got Selig to find you.

MARTHA. Where they at? (*Turns to BERTHA.*) They upstairs?

SETH. He was standing right up there on Manilla Street. I had to ask him to leave cause of how he was carrying on.

(*LOOMIS enters suddenly with ZONIA in hand. They cross rapidly through the parlor and into the kitchen.*)

SETH. He come in here one night ... (*SETH breaks off as LOOMIS comes into the kitchen. There is a long pause as MARTHA and LOOMIS look at each other.*)

LOOMIS. Hello, Martha.

MARTHA. (*Disbelieving.*) Herald?... (*Ecstatic.*) Zonia!

(*MARTHA rushes toward ZONIA. LOOMIS steps in front of ZONIA, blocking her path. ZONIA hides behind LOOMIS. MARTHA stops.*)

LOOMIS. You ain't waited for me, Martha. I got out the place looking to see your face. Seven years I waited to see your face.

MARTHA. Herald, I been looking for you. I wasn't but two months behind you when you went to my mama's and got Zonia. I been looking for you ever since.

LOOMIS. Joe Turner let me loose and I felt all turned around inside. I just wanted to see your face to know that the world was still there. Make sure everything still in its place so I could reconnect myself together. I got there and you was gone, Martha.

MARTHA. (*Steps in to him.*) Herald ...

LOOMIS. Left my little girl motherless in the world.

(*MARTHA recoils, goes to BERTHA for support. BERTHA gives her a reassuring look. MARTHA turns back to LOOMIS. MATTIE turns away.*)

MARTHA. I didn't leave her motherless, Herald. Reverend Tolliver wanted to move the church up North cause of all the trouble the colored folks was having down there. Nobody knew what was gonna happen traveling them roads. We didn't even know if we was gonna make it up here or not. I left her with my mama so she be safe. That was better than dragging her out on the road having to duck and hide from people. Wasn't no telling what was gonna happen to us. I didn't leave her motherless in the world. I been looking for you.

LOOMIS. I come up on Henry Thompson's place after seven years of living in hell, and all I'm looking to do is see your face.

MARTHA. (*Steps toward him. Gently and painfully.*) Herald, I didn't know if you was ever coming back. They told me Joe Turner had you and my whole world split half in two. My whole life shattered. It was like I had poured it in a cracked jar and it all leaked out the bottom. When it go like that there ain't nothing you can do to put it back together. You talking about Henry Thompson's place like I'm still gonna be there working the land by myself. How

I'm gonna do that? You wasn't gone but two months and Henry Thompson kicked me off his land and I ain't had no place to go but to my mama's I stayed and waited there for five years before I woke up one morning and decided that you was dead. Even if you weren't, you were dead to me. I wasn't gonna carry you with me no more. So I killed you in my heart. I buried you. I mourned you. And then I picked up what was left and went on to make life without you. I was a young woman with life at my beckon. I couldn't drag you behind me like a sack of cotton.

LOOMIS. *(Steps towards her.)* I just been waiting to look on your face to say my goodbye. That goodbye got so big at times, seem like it was gonna swallow me up. Like Jonah in the whale's belly I sat up in that goodbye for four years. That goodbye kept me out on the road searching. Not looking on women in their houses. It kept me bound up to the road. All the time the goodbye swelling up in my chest till I'm about to bust. Now that I see your face I can say my goodbye and make my own world. *(Turns, holds out his hand to ZONIA. She crosses to him, and takes his hand. He presents her to MARTHA.)* Martha ... here go your daughter. I tried to take care of her. See that she had something to eat. See that she was out of the elements. Whatever I know I tried to teach her. Now she need to learn from her mother whatever you got to teach her. That way she won't be no one-sided person. *(Crouches down, turns ZONIA to face him, his hands on her shoulders.)* Zonia, you go live with your mama. She a good woman. You go on with her and listen to her good. You my daughter and I love you like a daughter. I hope to see you again in the world somewhere. I'll never forget you.

(*LOOMIS rises, and kisses ZONIA on the forehead. He turns her to face MARTHA. MARTHA puts her Bible down on the bench. ZONIA crosses slowly to the bench, and puts down her bundle and hat. She turns suddenly to LOOMIS, runs to him, jumps up and throws her arms around his neck. He supports her as she clings to him. MARTHA turns away.*)

ZONIA. I won't get no bigger! My bones won't get no bigger! They won't! I promise! Take me with you till we keep searching and never finding. I won't get no bigger! I promise!
LOOMIS. (*Sets her down firmly.*) Go on and do what I told you now.

(*ZONIA slowly unclasps her arms. LOOMIS turns her toward MARTIIA, and gives her a gentle push.*)

MARTHA. (*Holds out her arms to ZONIA.*) It's alright, baby. Mama's here. Mama's here.

(*ZONIA suddenly runs to her. They embrace. LOOMIS turns away, crosses through the parlor to the front door. MARTHA breaks her embrace and dries ZONIA's tears with her handkerchief.*)

MARTHA. Don't worry. Don't cry. (*Turns to BYNUM.*) Mr. Bynum. I don't know how to thank you.

(*LOOMIS stops, turns suddenly and moves back into the kitchen, towards BYNUM.*)

MARTHA. God bless you.

(*BERTHA, MARTHA and ZONIA all hug in one big embrace.*)

LOOMIS. (*Accusingly.*) It was you! All the time it was you that bind me up! You bound me to the road!

BYNUM. I ain't bind you, Herald Loomis. You can't bind what don't cling.

LOOMIS. (*Turns away, distraught, crosses below the parlor table.*) Everywhere I go people wanna bind me up. Joe Turner wanna bind me up! Reverend Tolliver wanna bind me up. You wanna bind me up. Everybody wanna bind me up. Well, Joe Turner's come and gone and Herald Loomis ain't for no binding. (*Draws a hunting knife out of his coat pocket, raises it and starts towards BYNUM. ALL recoil.*) I ain't gonna let nobody bind me up!

BYNUM. (*Rises rapidly and backs away below the stove. SETH tries to shield him from behind.*) It wasn't you, Herald Loomis. I ain't bound you. I bound the little girl to her mother. That's who I bound.

(*LOOMIS stops short of the kitchen table.*)

BYNUM. You binding yourself. You bound onto your song. All you got to do is stand up and sing it, Herald Loomis. It's right there kicking at your throat. All you got to do is sing it. Then you be free.

MARTHA. (*Passes ZONIA to BERTHA, who embraces her and hides her face. MARTHA moves to the upstage right corner of the kitchen table. Fights for his soul.*) Herald ... look at yourself! Standing there with a knife in your hand. You done gone over to the devil. Comeon ... put down that knife. (*Steps down to the bench, picks up her Bible and holds aloft. Turns to the room at large and then to him.*) You got to look to Jesus. Even if you done fell away from the church you can be saved again. (*Holds the Bible out to him.*) The Bible say, "The Lord is my shepherd I shall not want. He maketh me to lie down in green pastures. He leads me beside the still water. He restoreth my soul. He leads me in the path of righteousness for His name's sake. Yea though I walk through the valley of the shadow of death ..." (*Continues to quote, testifies throughout the following LOOMIS lines.*)

LOOMIS. That's just where I be walking!

MARTHA. "I shall fear no evil. For Thou are with me. They rod and they staff, they comfort me."

LOOMIS. You can't tell me nothing about no valleys. I done been all across the valleys and the hills and the mountains and the oceans.

MARTHA. "Thous preparest a table before me in the presence of my enemies."

LOOMIS. All I seen was a bunch of niggers dazed out of their wooly heads. And Mr. Jesus Christ standing there in the middle of them, grinning.

MARTHA. "Thous anointest my head with oil, my cup runneth over."

LOOMIS. He grin that big old grin ... and niggers wallowing at his feet.

MARTHA. Surely goodness and mercy shall follow me all the days of my life, and I shall dwell in the house of the Lord forever." (*Continues to testify, no longer quoting from the Bible.*)

LOOMIS. Great big old white man ... your Mr. Jesus Christ. Standing there with a whip on one hand and tote board in another, and them niggers swimming in a sea of cotton. And he counting. He tallying up that cotton.

"Well, Jeremiah ... what's the matter you ain't picked but two hundred pounds of cotton today? Got to put you on half rations." and Jeremiah go back and lay up there on his half rations and talk about what a nice man Mr. Jesus Christ is cause he give him salvation after he die. Something wrong here. Something don't fit right!

MARTHA. You got to open up your heart and have faith, Herald. This world is just a trial for the next. (*Moves to downstage center.*) Jesus offers you salvation. (*Falls to her knees, holds the Bible out to LOOMIS.*)

LOOMIS. I been wading in the water. I been walking all over the river Jordan. But what it get me, huh?

(*LOOMIS crosses to MARTHA. SETH moves toward the stage right chair.*)

LOOMIS. I done been baptized with the blood of the lamb and the fire of the Holy Ghost. But what I git, huh? I got salvation? My enemies all around me picking the flesh from my bones. (*Backs away from her, clutches his chest, and tears his hand away.*) I'm choking on my own blood and all you got to give me is salvation?

MARTHA. (*Sure.*) You got to be clean, Herald. You got to be washed with the blood of the lamb.

LOOMIS. (*Crosses to her.*) Blood make you clean? You clean with blood?

MARTHA. Jesus bled for you.

LOOMIS. I don't need nobody to bleed for me! I can bleed for myself.

MARTHA. You got to be something, Herald. You just can't be alive. Live don't mean nothing unless it got a meaning.

LOOMIS. What kind of meaning you got? What kind of clean you got, woman? (*Backs to below the sliding door, and rips his shirt and vest open.*) You want blood? Blood make you clean? You clean with blood?

(*LOOMIS slashes himself across the chest. SETH and MATTIE move a step toward him in horror as he staggers back. SELIG recoils. BERTHA hides ZONIA's face. MARTHA and BYNUM look him in the eye. LOOMIS stands up, looks down at the blood on his chest, wipes his hands across his blood, washes the blood over his face in wonder, and looks down at his outstretched palms.*)

LOOMIS. I'm standing! (*Looks to BYNUM, drops the knife in his coat pocket.*) I'm standing. My legs stood up! (*Looks to MARTHA, who rises.*) I'm standing now!

(*Having found his song, the song of self-sufficiency, fully resurrected, cleansed and given breath, free from any encumbrance other than the workings of his own heart and the bonds of the flesh, having accepted the responsibility for his own presence in the world, he is free to soar above the environs that weight and push his spirit into terrifying contractions. LOOMIS crosses to MARTHA, touches her cheek with his hand in a caress as BERTHA releases ZONIA.*)

LOOMIS. Goodbye, Martha.

(*LOOMIS turns and exits through the front door, walking tall. MARTHA turns away and runs to embrace ZONIA. MATTIE looks to BERTHA for support.*

Finding it there, she picks up LOOMIS' hat, and rushes out after him. BERTHA moves to SETH.

BYNUM. Herald Loomis, you shining. You shining like new money!

(SETH puts his arm around BERTHA, and BYNUM nods as the LIGHTS: fade to black.)

END OF PLAY

COSTUME PLOT

BERTHA HOLLY

I. 1

Camisole: white cotton
Petticoat: white cotton with deep eyelet ruffle
House Dress: rose & lavender floral cotton on cream
    ground
Full Apron: light cream cotton with apple print and blue
    dots
Stockings: dark support hose
Shoes: brown high lace
Wedding Band: small gold
Wig: black
Headscarf: red w/ blue plaid

I. 3

Strike: Dress, Apron, Scarf
Add: House Dress: yellow cotton w/ large grey
    windowpane plaid
Half Apron: brown/mauve butterfly print
Scarf: beige floral print

I. 4

Strike: Dress, Apron, Scarf
Add: Skirt: blown wool w/ diagonal pleats and self buttons
Blouse: white cotton w/ pleating and insertion
Half Apron: white cotton w/ black ribbon insert
Brooch: russet cameo sewn to blouse
Haircombs: 2 tortoise shell
Handkerchief: with floral applique

II. 1
Strike: Skirt, Blouse, Apron, Haircombs, Handkerchief
Add: House Dress: yellow w/ grey windowpane plaid
Scarf: beige print

II. 3
Add: Half Apron: butterfly print

II. 5
Strike: Apron, Scarf
Add: Full Apron: apple print
Scarf: red/blue plaid

MATTIE CAMPBELL

I. 1
Camisole: off-white cotton w/ insertion
Petticoat: white taffeta
Blouse: cream w/ blue flowered print
Skirt: blue/green/brown plaid cotton
Stockings: white cotton lisle
Garters: leg garters at all times
Shoes: black lace up low boots
Gloves: tan linen
Purse: beige crocheted - pocket sewn inside for quarter
Handkerchief: white w/ yellow trim
Brooch: painted vignette
Wig: black
Hat: large straw w/ floral cotton band

I. 5
Strike: Blouse, Skirt, Hat, Gloves, Purse, Brooch

Add: Blouse: white w/ black dots
Shirt: white w/ blue and grey striped linen
Handkerchief: white w/purple flower in corner

II. 1
Repeat: Act I, Scene 1 (carry hat and purse, don't use
    gloves)

II. 2
Strike: Blouse, Skirt, Hat, Purse
Add: Blouse, white w/ lace trim
Skirt: blue glen plaid wool/linen
Overdress: nightgown: white cotton w/ lace trim and
    yellow bow

II. 3
Strike: Nightgown

II. 5
Strike: Blouse
Add: Blouse: cream w/ blue floral print (same as before)
MOLLY CUNNINGHAM

I. 4
Padded Bra: pink
Camisole: white cotton w/ insertion
Girdle: pink
Petticoat: black taffeta
Blouse: white embroidered cotton w/ eyelet trim
Jacket: maroon faille w/ grey trim and black buttons
Skirt: maroon faille to match
Stockings: pink silk
Garters: leg garters

Shoes: black lace-up low boots
Purse: black grosgrain - pocket sewed inside for quarter
Handkerchief: pink w /lace
Earrings: drop style, red stones
Gloves: long black silk marquisette
Wig: black
Hat: large black fur felt w/ black veiling & white plumes
Compact: in purse

I. 5
Strike: Jacket, Gloves, Hat, Purse

II. 1
Strike: Blouse, Skirt
Add: Blouse: white silk crepe w/ large lace collar
Skirt: maroon w/ blue and gold shadow plaid wool
MARTHA LOOMIS

II. 5
Camisole: white cotton
Petticoat: white cotton
Jacket: dark grey cotton w/ subtle grey tattersall plaid &
    off-white collar and cuffs
Skirt: dark grey cotton to match jacket
Tights: black cotton
Shoes: black lace-up low boots
Gloves: off-white cotton jersey
Hand bag: black velvet
Cross on Chain: gold
Handkerchief
Wig: black
Hat: large black soft felt, small brim
Bow Tie

ZONIA LOOMIS

I. 1
Camisole: white cotton
Bloomers: white cotton
Petticoat: white cotton
Dress: blue/white/yellow plaid cotton
Pinafore: faded blue gingham
Stockings: dark grey cotton lisle
Roll Garters
Shoes: brown distressed low lace-up boots (one pair for each girl)
Hat: straw w/ black grosgrain ribbon band and bow

I. 5
Strike: Pinafore

II. 1
Add: Pinafore

II. 4
Strike: Pinafore

II. 5
Strike: Dress
Add: Dress: white embroidered cotton w/ pleating & insertion
Costume Prop: Large White Ribbon Bow on Haircomb (1 + Back-up)

SETH HOLLY

I.1
Shirt: beige w/ grey and lavender stripe
Trousers: grey stripe
Belt: brown
Suspenders: brown w/ blue stripe
Socks: black
Shoes: brown lace-up high boots
Pocket Watch & Fob: old gold, pinned in to shirt
Wedding Ring: gold

I.3
Strike: Shirt, Trousers, Belt, Suspenders
Add: Shirt: white w/ grey stripe
Undershirt: with padded shoulders
Trousers: tan
Belt: brown
Suspenders: tan w/ brown stripe

I.4
Strike: Shirt, Trousers, Belt, Suspenders
Add: Trousers: brown glen plaid (from suit)
Suspenders: brown w/ grey stripe
Shaving Cream
Towel: white w/ green stripe

I.4 & 5
Strike: Undershirt
Add: Shirt: white w/ attached collar
Tie: green
Tie Tack: round, gold

Vest: brown glen plaid
Jacket: brown glen plaid to match
Pocket Watch w/ Fob: silver, clips into vest buttonhole
Handkerchief

II. 1
Strike: Suit, Shirt, Suspenders
Add: Shirt: white cotton w/ grey stripe
Trousers: dark green
Suspenders: brown w/ blue stripe
Pocket Watch: silver, pinned in to shirt

II. 1 (re-ent.)
Add: Apron: grey cotton
Gloves: work gloves w/ red stripe
Cap: grey/blue stripe
Goggles

II. 2
Strike: Shirt, Trousers
Add: Shirt: tan w/ lavender stripe
Trousers: tan

II. 3
Strike: Shirt, Trousers
Add: Shirt: blue and white striped
Trousers: grey trousers

II. 5
Strike: Shirt, Trousers
Add: Shirt: any other
Trousers: any other

JEREMY FURLOW

I, 1
Shirt: tan and brown stripe
Overalls: old blue denim, patched & faded
Socks: black
Shoes: black lace-up high boots
Bandana: old faded purple cotton
Cap: old grey tweed

I, 4
Strike: Shirt, Overalls, Bandana
Add: Shirt: white w/ attached collar
Tie: red w/ blue pattern
Jacket: blue w/ grey stripe
Trousers: blue w/ grey stripe to match
Suspenders: blue striped

II, 1
Strike: Shirt, Tie, Jacket, Trousers, Suspenders
Add: Repeat Act I, 1

BYNUM WALKER

I, 1
Shirt: white cotton
T-shirt
Tie: rust paisley
Vest: green herringbone tweed
Jacket: brown tweed
Trousers: brown wool patched

Suspenders: navy w/white edge
Socks: white athletic
Shoes: old brown lace-up high boots
Beads: black
Handkerchief
Tie Tack: silver square
Watch: silver w/ black ribbon, pinned to lapel
Hat: old distressed brown straw fedora

Costume Props: assorted silk flower boutonnieres

RUTHERFORD SELIG

I. 1
Shirt: white with red stripe
Bow Tie: maroon dotted
Vest: brown/green plaid wool
Jacket: brown wool
Trousers: dark grey wool
Suspenders: beige striped
Socks: black nylon
Shoes: brown distressed lace-up high boots
Pocket Watch & Fob: silver
Eyeglasses: gold round wire rims
Hat: brown felt fedora
T-shirt
Handkerchief
Extra white shirt

HERALD LOOMIS

I, 1
Shirt: pink/white cotton w/ collar
Tie: black
Vest: black wool
Jacket: black wool to match
Trousers: black wool
Suspenders: black
Overcoat: dark grey wool
Socks: dark cotton
Knee pads: athletic heavy duty, large
Shoes: black distressed lace-up high boots
Elbow pads: athletic heavy duty, large
Ace Bandage: 2" velcro closure strong support
Wrist brace: velcro closure, strong support
Hat: distressed black felt fedora
Underwear
Buttons on elastic for neck
Stud

REUBEN MERCER

I, 1
Shirt: olive striped collarless cotton
Knickers: brown patched corduroy, leg cuffs unsnapped
Suspenders
Socks: olive cotton
Shoes: old brown lace-up high boots
T-shirt

COSTUME PRESETS
TOP OF SHOW

SETH	Brown Suit Jacket	SR Quick Change Booth
"	Vest w/ Pocket Watch	"
"	White Shirt	"
"	Green Tie (pre-tied)	"
"	Brown Suit Trousers	"
BERTHA	White Pleated Blouse	Wardrobe in Bedroom
"	Brown Wool Skirt	"
"	White Apron	"
"	2 Haircombs	"

INTERMISSION

ZONIA	White Dress	Close to Bedroom
"	Straw Hat	"
SETH	Tan Trousers	SR Quick Change Booth
"	Tan Striped Shirt w/ Pocket Watch	"
"	Grey Striped Trousers	"
"	Navy & White Stripe Shirt	"

PROPERTY LIST

Furniture:

Sink: 54"W x 22"D x 35"H - porcelain, large sink opening with attached drainboard, two faucets, exposed pipes, s-curve drainpipe should be mounted as close to underside of drain as possible to allow room underneath. Running water must drain off.

Icebox: 24"W x 20"D x 37"H - wood, painted white, brass hardware: 2 doors hinged on left side, 1 on top, 1 on bottom.

UR Small Table: 23"W x 18"D x 30"H - wood

Stove: 35"W x 27"D x 65"H - enamel on steel, painted beige: upper warming oven with 2 side-by-side compartments; middle shelf at back is 6" D over the 6 burner stove; oven below has 1 door hinged at right side and contains two shelves.

UC Small Table: 23"W x 17"D x 33"H - wood.

Kitchen Table: 84"W x 30"D x 30"H - wood, painted beige: top is 1 and 1/2" planking.

Bench: 75"W x 12"D x 16"H - wood, painted beige to match kitchen table.

5 Side Chairs: 3 Tall Pressback: 18"W x 17"D x 40"H - oak; 2 Shorter Pressback: 18"W x 17"D x 36"H - oak.

Dressing:
1) Pink Geranium in Clay Pot
2) 4 Folded Brown Paper Grocery Bags
3) Tall Milk Can
4) Dried Herbs: (6 bunches assorted kinds)
5) Dried Chilis: on a string
6) Bee Smoker
7) Oil Lamp: milk glass with clear glass chimney

8) Potato Ricer
9) Rectangular Wooden Box w/ Lid: painted white
10) Coal Bucket (full of coal)
11) 1 White Ceramic Crock
12) 1 White Ceramic Jug w/ Handle
13) 1 Brown Ceramic Crock
14) Roller Towel: loop towel mounted on metal roller
15) Small Mirror: 8" x 10"
16) Bar of White Ivory Soap: bath size
17) Bar of Fels Naptha Soap
18) Brown/White Checked Dishtowel
19) Washtub with Mounted Wringer: must fit under sink
    between deck and s-curve of drainpipe and slide in and
    out easily, felt bottom to deaden sound
20) Round Metal Trashcan
21) Paper Bag: (one each performance) grocery size - to fit
    in trashcan
22) Baking Pan lined w/ felt 13" x 9" x 2", felt should
    match color of pan
23) 2 semi-ripe Plastic Tomatoes/1 Green Plastic Tomato:
    should be weighted with birdseed or sand
24) Metal Flour Cannister with Lid
25) Wooden Spoon
26) Flour
27) Baking Powder Tin
28) Large Wooden Bowl
29) Clear Glass Whiskey Bottle: label off - used for rolling
    pin
30) Rag
31) S & P Shakers: cut-glass, filled with salt and pepper,
    should be square shaped so that if knocked over they
    will not roll off table
32) Butter Dish: cut-glass, lid used for storage only

33) Stick of Butter
34) Butter Knife
35) Sugar Bowl with Lid
36) 2 Pot Holders
37) Small Metal Ashtray
38) Spatula
39) Cast Iron Pot with Lid: dutch oven 8" diameter base, 10" diameter at top
40) Round Cake Pan: to line inside cast iron pot - 8" diameter - holds applesauce
41) Applesauce: 25 oz. per performance
42) Wooden Spoon w/ Hooked Handle
43) Cast Iron Skillet: 10" size
44) Brown Gravy
45) Wooden Spoon
46) Coffee Pot #1: standard camp stove-type, blackened as if old - must hold at least 6 cups of coffee
47) Instant Tea w/ lemon: iced tea mix
48) Food Coloring
49) 2 Biscuit Pans: black metal deep-dish pizza pans, 10" diam.
50) Biscuits (12 biscuits per performance)
51) 6 Bowls
52) 6 Small Plates
53) 6 Coffee Cups

IN PARLOR

Furniture:

Parlor Rug: 8' x 10' - wool oriental: navy blue with rose accents, short off-white fringe on ends.
Round Table: 30"D x 30"H - wood stained dark: base is footed pedestal
Upholstered Armchair: 22"W x 20"D x 40"H (seat 18"H) - frame wood: stained dark; seat and back upholstered in rose damask.
Upholstered Side Chair: 19"W X 18"D X 33"H (Seat 19"H) - Frame wood: stained dark to match armchair; seat and back upholstered in rose damask. Front legs on caster wheels.
Love seat: 48"W x 19"D x 37"H (seat 19"H) - frame wood: stained dark to match two chairs; seat and back upholstered in rose damask.

Dressing:

54) Tablecloth: square, rose & Maroon damask, fringed on all sides, to fit round parlor table, stitch cord on underside to fit table edge
55) Oval Portrait of Miss Mabel: w/ wooden frame
56) Braided Valance: maroon, hung w/ wooden rings

Hand Props:

57) ROOMS TO LET Sign: wooden, hand-lettered with hanger wire attached
58) Glued Domino Game: a domino game in progress, glued together

59) 17 Loose Domino Tiles: (incl. 3 x 1/5 tiles)

IN BEDROOM

Furniture:

Wardrobe: 24" x 24" x 84", tall wooden closet, open (no door), with clothes rack inside
Bed: abnormally small, not used

Dressing:
60) 2 Hat Boxes: different shapes and sizes
61) Bedspread, Underskirt: different fabrics
62) 3 Pillows: various sizes, fabric covers

IN PANTRY:

Furniture:

Wooden Shelf Unit: 36"W x 12"D x 104"H - painted white, has 6 shelves - each one 15"H; no base, unit rests on floor with floor as bottom shelf (not included in shelf count).
Cupboard: 44 3/4"W x 16"D x 103"H: 3 doors over head, counter over two drawers below: - painted off-white with pale green trim: cupboard above has two shelves inside 15"H, drawers below are not functional

Hand Props:
63) 3 Folded White Flat Sheets
64) Sewing Basket: wicker lined with fabric
65) in: Navy Blue Sock w/ hole
66)   in: Darning Egg: wooden

67)   Pincushion: red stuffed tomato
68)   in: Threaded Needle
69)   Straight Pins
70) Scissors: small pair of sewing scissors
71)   Spool of Black Thread: wax coated thread
72) Sock Dressing: 6 extra socks balled up
73) Washboard: wooden
74) 6 Medium Plates
75) 6 Silverware Sets: 1 set = 1 knife & 1 spoon, rolled in
    1 napkin

Dressing:(listed for shelf unit from top to bottom)
76) Square Wicker Basket w/ lid
77) Large Oval Wicker Basket
78) Small Metal Whitman Box w/ lid
79) 1 Tall Tin w/ Lid painted white
80) Wooden Dustpan
81) Iron
82) Funnel-shaped Strainer
83) Teapot
84) Muffin Tin
85) Cedar Box
86) Rectangular Wicker Basket w/ Lid and Handle: picnic
    hamper
87) Small Woven Oval Basket
88) Large Rectangular Wooden Box w/ Lid
89) Large Oval Wicker Basket with handles: laundry basket
90) Rectangular Metal Pail w/ handle
91) Metal Bread Box: white enamel with red lid
92) Large Metal Dipper
93) Bundt Pan
94) White Enamel Metal Baking Pan
95) 1 Tall Tin w/ Lid: painted white

96) Metal Grater: standing kind
97) White Ceramic Flower Pot
98) Long Wooden Box w/ Lid: painted white
99) 3 Cannister Set: various sizes, glass with wooden lids, 1 each filled w/ dried kidney beans, rice, dried green peas
100) Large Square Wicker Basket w/ Lid
101) 3 Folded Lace Scraps: assorted kinds and colors
102) Small Glass Cookie Jar: painted white
103) Large Metal Colander: painted white

Stage Right Presets: – Actor Prop Table
104) 6 Sheets of Sheet Metal: 18" x 18"
105) Bynum's Basket: dark wicker, no handle, with florist foam insert covered with burlap inside - attach pocket along one edge at top inside to hold unsewn packet
106)   in: Pigeon Blood Cup: metal with lid, should be painted to look bloody
107)   Small Brown Paper Bundle: tied with string
108)   Assorted Green and Brown Weeds
109)   4 Cloth Packets 1 1/2" x 2" muslin folded over and sewn at top, fill with straw
110)   in basket pocket: Unsewn Packet: fill with straw, fold over top
111)   in: Threaded Needle (12" long black thread, knotted at end)
112) 2 Cat's Cradle Strings: white soft cord
113) Reuben's Stuff: 5 Jacks, 4 Rubber Bands, 2 Dice, 1 Finger Puppet, 2 Checkers, 1 Blue Ribbon, 1 Small Spring
114) 6 Pots on a String: aluminum with handles, various sizes, each should fit inside the next, hole drilled

through end of handles, twine goes through each hole
to tie up on loop
115) Sack of Vegetables: burlap bag, w/ attached arm strap,
holds 6 cabbages and sugar bag of 6 tomatoes
116) 6 Plastic Cabbages: weighted with sand or birdseed
117) Sm Sugar Bag: muslin cloth, 5# size
118) 4 Plastic Tomatoes: ripe looking, must be weighted
with birdseed or sand
119) Lunch Pail: aluminum with handle and lid
120) Seth's Work Gloves
121) Seth's Hat
122) Seth's goggles
123) Seth's Apron
124) Metal Bucket
125) Rag

For Shifts
126) Cutting Board: wood, 14" x 20"
127) White Playdough
128) Clean Cloth
129) Sm Faceted Glass
130) Biscuit Pan w/ 6 Raw Biscuits: black deep dish pizza
pan, as in first description, biscuits are cutouts of
white playdough
131) Coffee Pot #2: matches first pot, but looks new - as
if made from sheet metal
132) Shaving Mug
133)   in: Cake of Shaving Soap
134) Shaving Brush
135) Razor: folding straight razor
136) Kitchen Tablecloth: off-white damask, stick corners in
to fit kitchen table, on 1 end attach safety pin with
glo-tape to mark corners

137) Tin Bowl: enamel on tin, large serving size
138) 2 Glasses: tumblers, straight side standard
139) Lemon Gatorade: 1 glass total, divided usage
140) Dirty Platter: serving platter painted to look dirty
141) Stack of 7 "Dirty" Plates: dinner size painted to look dirty
142) White Potato Bowl: white china, painted with textured paint to look like mashed potato leftovers
143) Wooden Spoon
144) 2 Small Plates
145) 2 Loose Spoons
146) Loose Napkin
147) 3 Silverware Sets
148) 5 Cups
149) "Dirty" Milk Glass: inside bottom painted to look like milk
150) Granulated Sugar
151) 2 Qt. Milk Pail: metal with handle and lid
152) Small Plate
153) Baked Yam
154) Folded Napkin
155) Fork
156) Glass: straight side tumbler
157) Small Plate
158) 1 Cup
159) Napkin
160) Knife
161) Bowl
162) Small Plate
163) 1 Cup
164) Silverware Set
165) Small Plate
166) 1 Empty Milk Glass:

UC Quick Change Booth
167) Shaving Cream
168) White Towel w/ Green Stripe: bath size towel
169) Broom: old-fashioned, straw bound with twine to handle
170)   glued to: extra twine
171)   wrapped around: twig

Stage Left Presets: Actor's Prop Table
172) Zonia's Bundle: large square of fabric stuffed with clothes, tie corners across diagonal to each other
173) Guitar: old, battered, 6-string; steel strings; is not played on stage
174) Suitcase: nice, leather, period
175) 2- White Ribbon Bow on Haircomb
176) 1 Pillow Case
177) 5 Flat White Sheets

Dressing Room Presets
178) 30 Oversized Dollar Bills: period paper money was larger than present day - year is 1911
179) Small Bible: black cover
180) 12 Quarters or Shillings
181) Meerschaum Pipe
182) Cherry Tobacco
183) Small Boxes of Wooden Matches
184) 3 Small Notebooks: assorted sizes and colors
185) 4 Pencils: whittled points
186) Leather Shoulder Bag: with long strap, outside flap pocket to hold money, inside zippered compartment

ACT II Prop Table

187) Blood Knife (fill with blood mixture and cap with
     Vaseline
188) 2 Blood Packs (fill corner of baggie with 2T. blood
     mixture and twist tie tightly with no air pocket, clip
     twist tie ends off)

Total Number of:
Small Plates - 12
Medium Plates - 6
Bowls - 7
Coffee Cups - 13
Napkins - 13
Knives - 11
Forks - 2
Spoons - 12
Lemonade Glasses - 3

Perishables Used Per Show:
1 Whole Yam: unpeeled, scrubbed, baked
10 oz Glass Lemon Gatorade: divided usage
1/3 Stick Butter
25 oz Applesauce
12 Biscuits: trim with glass, cut bottom off of 10
12 cups Ice Tea w/ Lemon Mix and food coloring as needed
to make coffee color
1 Jar Brown Gravy: replace as needed - dressing
3 T. Sugar
Salt: as needed
Flour: as needed
1 Can White Playdough

Blood Recipe
1/2 cup KMS Styling Gel*
1/8 cup cold water
1 Tbsp. ERA Liquid Detergent*
1/4 tsp. Red Food Color
1 1/2 drops Blue Food Color

Add 1/8 cup cold water to 1/2 cup styling gel. Stir to mix completely. Add 1T of ERA. Stir. Mixture should be consistency of lumpy syrup. Add red food color, stir well. Add blue food color, stir well. If recipe sits too long it will thicken up. Make at top of show to avoid this problem.

---

* These brands are very important in terms of the consistency and washability of the blood recipe. KMS is the only green styling gel which contains lanolin, and ERA is a dark blue detergent which allows us to use less food coloring. KMS is available through professional beauty supply stores. If ERA is not available in your area, SOLO has been used as a substitute.

ONSTAGE PRESETS

Kitchen:

Sink: Water on.
<u>Hanging Over</u>: Roller Towel, Mirror
<u>On Drainboard</u>: Bar of Ivory Soap, Bar of Fels Naptha Soap, Dish Towel (brown checked)
<u>In DR corner of Basin</u>: Shaving Mug with Shaving Brush in, Razor (open, blade pointing offstage, glotape up)
<u>Under</u>: Washtub, on DR end: Wringer; Leaning in: Baking Pan lined with felt; Trashcan, in: Paper Bag (roll down top)
Fridge: <u>On DR corner</u>: Geranium in clay pot; around pot: 2 semi-ripe tomatoes (DL & US of pot); 1 Green tomato (DS w/ ripe as pair)
<u>In Bottom Compartment</u>: Milk Pail (lid for offstage storage only); in: 2 cups of reconstituted powdered Milk

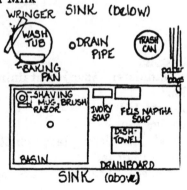

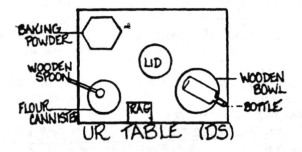

UR Small Table:
On: Flour Cannister (open) containing wooden spoon & flour
Flour Cannister Lid
Baking Powder Tin
Wooden Bowl in: Clear glass whiskey bottle (lightly dusted w/ flour)
Rag (damp, folded), hanging over DS edge of table

Stove

Oh Shelf: Salt & Pepper Shakers
Butter Dish (lid for offstage storage only) on:
Stick of Butter, Butter Knife
Sugar Bowl (1/4 full of sugar)
2 Pot Holders
Ashtray
Spatula

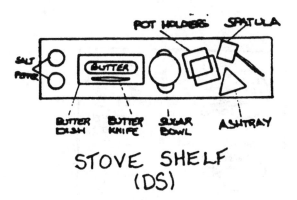

STOVE SHELF
(DS)

<u>On Burners</u>: Cast Iron Pot (UR) containing: Cake
Pan Liner containing: 28 oz Applesauce on: Lid
Skillet (DR) in: Brown Gravy, Wooden Spoon
Coffee Pot #1 (darker pot) (UL) containing:
Lipton Instant Tea/Lemon (5 cups), Food Coloring
(to make coffee color)
<u>In Oven</u>: 2 Biscuit Pans : in: 6 biscuits each (trim
w/ water glass)

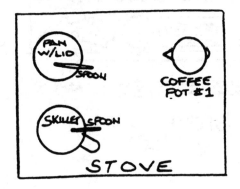

UC Small Table

On: 6 Bowls, 6 Small Plates, 6 Cups (2 stacks of 3)

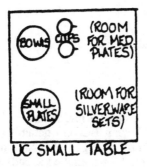

UC SMALL TABLE

Rug (check stapled down)
Round Table on: Tablecloth
Armchair
Side Chair (on glotape spikes)
Love Seat

Sliding Door pulled DS
Front Door Closed
Bedroom Door Closed
SR Window Closed

Pantry

On Second Shelf: 3 Folded White Sheets
On Third Shelf: Sewing Basket containing: Navy Blue
Sock w/hole; Darning Egg; Pincushion containing
Threaded Needle (12" long, knotted at end) Straight Pins;
Scissors, Spool of Black Thread, Socks Dressing
On All Shelves: Dressing
Leaning UR Corner: Washboard
On Small Table: 6 Medium Plates with 6 Silverware Sets
(1 set - 1 knife & 1 spoon rolled in 1 napkin)

Stage Right Presets - Actor Prop Table

8 Sheets of Sheet Metal
Bynum's Basket containing Pigeon Blood Cup (glued
down); Small Brown Paper Bundle; Weeds, 4 Cloth
Packets (in pocket:) Unsewn Packet containing Threaded
Needle (12" long, knotted at end)
Bynum's Hat
2 Cat's Cradle Strings (1 back-up)

Reuben's Stuff: 2 Rubber Bands, 1 Finger Puppet, 2 Dice, 5 Jacks, 1 Nickel, 1 Blue Ribbon, 1 Small Spring, 1 Empty Match Box
6 Pots on a String
Sack of Vegetables
Sm. Sugar Sack containing 2 Tomatoes
Two Ripe Tomatoes
Lunch Pail containing Lid, Seth's Gloves
Seth's Hat
Seth's Goggles
Seth's Apron
Bucket with Rag inside
Extra Dollar Bills (5)
Extra Boxes of Wooden Matches (2)

OFFSTAGE RIGHT PRESENTS FOR SHIFTS

For Shift #1: Act I Scene 2 to Act I Scene 3
Cutting Board containing: Flour (sprinkled lightly on board); White Playdough (ball & cut-out); Clean Cloth (folded); Sm. Glass (upside down); Biscuit Pan w/ 6 Raw Biscuits (dried playdough)
Coffee Pot #2 (silver one) containing Instant Lipton Tea w/Lemon (3 cups), Food Coloring (to make coffee color)

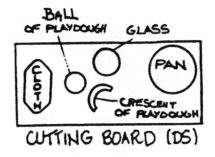

CUTTING BOARD (DS)

For Shift #3: Act I Scene 4 to Act I Scene 5
Kitchen Tablecloth (accordion fold)
Tin Bowl
1 Glass Tumbler
1 Glass Tumbler containing 1/4 glass of Lemon Gatorade
"Dirty" Platter containing Biscuit Crumb (from Shit #1)
Stack of 7 "Dirty" Plates
White Potato Bowl with Wooden Spoon in it

For Shift #4: Act II Scene 1 to Act II Scene 2
Small Plate on which is Baked Yam (cook during Juba
scene) place on a folded napkin
Fork
Glass Tumbler containing 3/4 glass of Lemon Gatorade

For Shift #5: Act II Scene 2 to Act II Scene 3
Small Plate
1 Coffee Cup
Napkin
Biscuit Pan with 1 biscuit
Bowl with 1 serving applesauce

For Shift #6: Act II Scene 4 to Act II Scene 5
Small Plate
1 Coffee Cup
Silverware Set
Small Plate containing 1 serving applesauce
1 Empty Milk Glass

Offstage Right Preset for Intermission Shift
Dishpan in which is: 2 small plates, 2 spoons, Loose
Napkin, 3 Silverware Sets, 5 Coffee Cups, "Dirty" Milk
Glass

Biscuit Pan containing 6 biscuits (from previous shifts)
Tray on which is Dominoes & Domino Game
3 Cups "Coffee" (Lipton Instant Tea w/ Lemon & Food
Coloring
Seth's Gloves

UC Quick Change Booth
Broom with extra twine glue to it, wrapped around twig
Pillowcase containing 3 rumpled sheets

Stage Left Presets - Actor's Prop Table
Zonia's Bundle (tied tightly)
Zonia's Hat
Suitcase
2 White Ribbon on Haircomb
Extra Dollar Bills (6)

Dressing Room Presets
MATTIE CAMPBELL: Crocheted Purse with 1 quarter in
pocket
MARTHA PENTECOST: Black Velvet Purse, Bible
MOLLY CUNNINGHAM: Black Beaded purse w/ 1 quarter
in pocket, Roll of Dollar Bills (12)
JEREMY FURLOW: 2 Dollar Bills, Guitar
HERALD LOOMIS: 3 Dollar Bills
RUTHERFORD SELIG: 14 Dollar Bills, 8 Assorted
Coins, Meerschaum Pipe, Cherry Tobacco, Box of Wooden
Matches, 3 Notebooks, 6 Pencils, Leather Shoulder Bag

JOE TURNER.

1. They tell me Joe Turner's come and gone (Oh Lordy) They tell me Joe
2. Come with forty links of chain (etc.)

Turner's come and gone (Oh Lordy) Got my man and gone.

AUGUST WILSON is a member of New Dramatists, Inc. and an Associate Playwright at the Playwrights Center in Minneapolis. He is a recipient of Bush, McKnight and Rockefeller Foundation Fellowships in playwriting. *Ma Rainey's Black Bottom** was presented by Yale Repertory Theatre as part of their 1983-84 season, and subsequently had a substantial Broadway run. *Fences* was presented on Broadway during the 1986-87 season, where it won every major award, including the Tony and the Pulitzer Prize. *Joe Turner's Come and Gone** also originated at Yale Rep and also had a substantial Broadway run. Mr. Wilson continued his association with Yale Rep with *The Piano Lesson** which opened on Broadway in 1990, winning another Pulitzer Prize for its author.

Mr. Wilson is also a poet and has published poems in various magazines and anthologies. He was born in Pittsburgh, Pennsylvania, and now lives in St. Paul, Minnesota.